Québec in the Duplessis Era, 1935-1959: Dictatorship or Democracy?

ISSUES IN CANADIAN HISTORY

General Editor
J. L. GRANATSTEIN

ISSUES
IN
CANADIAN
HISTORY

Québec in the Duplessis Era, 1935-1959: Dictatorship or Democracy?

Selected, edited and translated by
CAMERON NISH

THE COPP CLARK PUBLISHING COMPANY
TORONTO

To STEPHEN ABBOTT and his friend
Jean-Paul Nish

ISBN 0-7730-3114-6

Printed and bound in Canada

Preface

Many people have contributed to the elaboration of this book. I am very grateful to them. Jean-Pierre Gagnon, a history student at Laval University, patiently culled the many periodicals and newspapers containing material on Duplessis and Québec. His work under Professor Jean Hamelin of the same institution was an invaluable aid. Gilles Marsolais printed-off and filed all of the extracts, a very useful contribution.

Herbert (Herb) Quinn, Professor of Political Science at Sir George Williams University, made available to me his valuable collection of clippings and brochures on Quebec politics. The use I made of them expresses my gratitude.

The manuscript was prepared by Miss Nicole Bellemare, one of the secretaries of the Centre de Recherche en Histoire Economique du Canada français, a research institution supported jointly by l'Ecole des Hautes Etudes Commerciales and Sir George Williams University. As usual, her work was excellent, and she met the exigencies of the editor with unfailing good humour.

The committee for the Advancement of Scholarly Activities (CASA) of Sir George Williams University greatly assisted in the gathering of materials and the preparation of the book. Their never failing generosity was manifested by a grant in the summer of 1968.

Stephen Abbott, to whom this work is dedicated, as well as to his friend Jean-Paul, revised all the translations as well as the introductory narratives. For this, and his many other services, I am in his debt.

My Copp Clark editor, Tilly Crawley, is simply described. She is the best editor I have ever had.

Cameron Nish

Montréal, July 22, 1969.

Contents

Introduction

Maurice Le Noblet Duplessis had a decisive effect on Québec society. He was *Premier Ministre* of his native province from 1936 to 1939 and from 1944 till his death in September 1959. He implemented a political style called *Duplessisme*. There is little disagreement about these basic facts.

However, interpretations of the Duplessis era differ widely; Duplessis was always a controversial figure, in life and after his death. Many commentators view him as a power-hungry, corrupt dictator born on ". . . the same day as Hitler." The late André Laurendeau, while editor of *Le Devoir*, characterised Duplessis as a *roi nègre*, a Negro king. A leader of the provincial Liberal Party during the Duplessis reign, Georges-Emile Lapalme, depicted the leader of the government as a shrewd, crude, arbitrary, and sometimes convivial man. Paul Sauvé, one of Duplessis' ministers and briefly his successor, was seen to shrug his shoulders in despair over his *Chef's* actions. Pierre Elliott Trudeau attributed Duplessis' successes to the anti-democratic trends in Québec's political and social heritage. In this view he is supported by Herbert F. Quinn, a political scientist who attributed the success of Duplessis' electoral machine to patronage, telegraphing votes, and ward politics at their crudest. Totalitarian, dictatorial, and corrupt briefly describe this view of Québec in the Duplessis era. Yet in his time the Union Nationale held clear majorities of 62, 5, 72, 44 and 52 seats in the Legislative Assembly of Québec.

The electoral victories of the Union Nationale in 1936, 1944, 1948, 1952 and 1956 are inadequately explained by the hypothesis that the regime was totalitarian and dictatorial. The equation of Duplessis with the Union Nationale made in his lifetime and since his death begs the question of the party's success at the polls in 1966, after the era of the Quiet Revolution and the Lesage government.

The Union Nationale's stand on Federal-Provincial relations, property, business, labour, State-Church relations, and education are assumed to have been dictated by Duplessis' personal biases. Yet it was the Québec electorate that gave the mandate to Duplessis, the Union Nationale and its policies. The Duplessis era, therefore, could justly be explained by interpreting not Duplessis alone, but his society as well.

To say that a people get the government they deserve is a cliché. Is it equally trite to ask if a society gets the political parties it wants? It is a truism of history, so obvious that it is often overlooked, that a man and his society are two sides of the same coin. Our task is to examine Duplessis *and* Québec; the man *and* his society. Our purpose is to measure the influence of Duplessis on Québec and Québec on Duplessis. Only by examining Duplessis in context can informed views of the dictatorial or democratic nature of Québec in the Duplessis era be formed.

In Québec, Canada and the world, the 1930's were a period of change and contrasts. As a result of the First World War, many ethnic groups had been granted a new political expression in Europe: that of nation-states. Self-determination was a byword enshrined in Wilson's Fourteen Points and the Treaty of Versailles. Anti-Imperialism and ethnic nationalism were natural consequences of First World War slogans. The trauma of war had heightened Québec's self-consciousness. Conscription, the Union government and the Easter Riots in Québec City in 1917-1918 had increased tensions and exacerbated the racial cleavage in Québec and Canada. And shortly after the war, the abbé Lionel Groulx formed and led a separatist movement advocating a Laurentian State for the French Canadians.

The contrasts in the post-war world were striking. Prosperity and run-away inflation were followed by a world-wide depression. Bread lines, free soup kitchens and public relief were the palliatives offered to the unemployed. The depression of the 1930's was not merely economic; it was psychological as well. Belief and trust in the old order were casualties. The high hopes of the 1920's had been followed only by despair. Inevitably, the new and desperate conditions produced new and desperate options, and among those chosen in Europe were Mussolini's Fascism, Hitler's National Socialism, Salazar's Corporatism and Spain's Falangist doctrine.

Canada was not isolated from these varied responses to the depression. R. B. Bennett, the Conservative Prime Minister, proposed a radical New Deal for Canada only to find that his solution was *ultra vires.* The British North America Act 1867 and its amendments were inadequate to meet the exigencies of the 1930's. In Alberta, William (Bible Bill) Aberhart led his Social Credit party to power in 1935. The Regina Manifesto of 1933 became the charter of the Cooperative Commonwealth Federation, the first truly socialist party in Canada, and a landmark in Canadian political history. The CCF's achievements at the polls, however, were less than spectacular. The Liberal and Conservative parties continued bottling old wine in new bottles, and the economic crisis continued.

Responses in Québec were varied and complicated. In some ways this most traditional of traditional provinces was a microcosm of world options. A rigid, conservative Catholicism was challenged by a Catholic left. A nascent Communist movement was paralleled by nascent Nazi and Fascist movements. Corporatism had its Québec adherents. Canadian Federalism was supported by some and challenged by others.

Several varieties of separatism vied with each other, although all shared common views on Ottawa's nefarious role. It was in this maelstrom of ideologies that the Union Nationale was born.

In 1935 and 1936 the Québec electorate, interest groups, and institutions such as business, labour and the Church responded in a variety of ways to the stimuli of their times. One product of this era was Maurice Duplessis, and he became one of the few Depression politicians who managed to consolidate a political position and outlast the 1930's. Elections were held no less than eight times during his period of political prominence. In this book of readings we are seeking some of the political explanations of the Duplessis phenomenon.

The evidence is incomplete. For example, the Duplessis and Paul Gouin collections are not yet available for consultation. Other private and public archives are closed. Some of the evidence, perhaps most, reveals the biases of the writers, interest groups or institutions. Newspapers and periodicals were for or against Duplessis, rarely neutral. The *Montreal Gazette*, representative of the conservative-capitalist establishment, generally approved, as did the *Jesuit Relations*, and the extreme nationaliste paper *Action Nationale*. Radical periodicals such as the *Canadian Forum* viewed him as a *bête noir* because they saw him as a crypto-fascist dictator.

The story is not closed: this is but one chapter concerned with Duplessis' rise to power, the policies that were implemented in his lifetime, and personal assessments of the man and his effects on his society. Oddly enough, in these days of sociological explanation, the cult of personality dominates the explanations of Duplessis and his era; this interpretation is here confronted by an interpretation of the society that produced Maurice Duplessis and the Union Nationale.

Clash of Opinion

The deputy from Three Rivers has introduced into Parliamentary debates a polemical tone marked by spirit, dignity and gentility. Although he can be biting when the opportunity arises, he always stays within certain bounds. He prides himself on "never hitting an opponent below the belt." He is reluctant to use certain weapons, a restraint which some of his less scrupulous supporters hold against him.

L'Action Nationale

One of the pleasing features of Mr. Duplessis is that even his hottest opponents pay high tribute to his personal honesty. He is an upright man. Naturally, the Liberals allege that the iniquities which his government is presently perpetrating outrun anything which the Taschereau régime achieved even in its palmiest, or rather its palmoiliest, days. But it is really impossible to believe that anything could equal, let alone surpass, in this regard the Government which Duplessis over-threw.

ANDREW D. SAVAGE

The Union Nationale's victory marks, for the first time in the history of our province, the complete dissociation of provincial parties from federal parties . . . I will even go so far as to say that, if Duplessis keeps his promise to implement the Action Nationale program, provincial policies will soon come into such conflict with the federal government that the Union Nationale will either lead us straight to separatism, to the creation of a free French State in America, or Duplessis in turn will fall from power.

PAUL BOUCHARD

It is common belief in many sections of Canada and the United States that the Province of Quebec is advancing rapidly along the road to Fascism, and is only awaiting the appearance of a *Führer* who will set up a totalitarian dictatorship on the banks of the St. Lawrence, dissolve all political parties, crush the labour unions, regiment industry, liquidate all Communists, Socialists and Liberals, and establish a Corporative State, all with the approval if not the actual support of the Roman Catholic hierarchy in the province.

H. F. QUINN

There are some who, for what seems to us to be excellent reasons, think that the British North America Act is a treaty of union between two great races; others are of the opinion that it is only a law. I firmly believe that Confederation is a treaty of union between two great races.

MAURICE DUPLESSIS

As for the "compact theory" of Confederation, it is doubtful whether the masses of people, whether French-speaking or not, are aware of its implications if once thoroughly accepted as the nature of the Canadian federal union.

WILFRID EGGLESTON

The action of the Province of Quebec in prohibiting the granting of any rights in connection with Quebec Crown lands to any company not incorporated in that Province appears to us to be extremely unwise, extremely detrimental to the growth of National unity in Canada, and quite certain to provoke reprisals of a kind which will harm business interests in the Province itself and promote a general feeling of antagonism between Provinces throughout the Dominion.

Saturday Night

Quebec, the largest of Canada's provinces, within three years achieved the lowest per capita debt, with the single exception of the Province of Alberta. The new government has also effected sociological reforms in pensions and such matters, and started a vast highway construction program.

Monetary Times

Gradually to bring its wage and living standards into line with those in the rest of Canada seems to be the labor policy of the Quebec government. This is one phase of the modernistic trend in Quebec, which became evident when the Duplessis administration came into power in 1936. Other steps include new highways, a provincial power scheme, and rural credits. While such measures seem merely to follow paths already trodden by other provinces, the Quebec government has revealed, on a few matters, a reluctance to follow slow but sure methods, a desire to over-ride obstacles by methods which some critics call autocratic. The task of making over a people who have been schooled to cling to the past can not be easy.

WILLIAM WESTON

Where these syndicates do not exist, our Catholic workers will almost inevitably be organized into neutral unions. In the latter, there are apt to be leaders who are communists or who have communist tendencies. In this case, it is indispensable that our workers be organized in addition into confessional groups. For many years, the Holy See has requested this of them. Since these organizations cannot aim directly at union activity—inasmuch as union activity is in the hands of a neutral or foreign leadership—these Catholic organizations must be conceived of differently. . . .

JOSEPH H. LEDIT, s.j.

One of the most important prejudices in the mind of Quebec's nationalist Maurice Duplessis is his deep-rooted hatred of international labor unions. If the Quebec premier had his way, these "outside" labor organizations, whether of the AF of L, the CIO or the railway brotherhoods, would be banned in Quebec, and replaced by locally controlled unions of the Catholic Syndicate type. As long as federal wartime labor regulations were in effect, Premier Duplessis did not feel free to commence his "anti-foreign union" crusade—but judging by recent indications, this crusade will be announced any day now.

L. J. ROGERS

The Witnesses, like a good many other earnest fanatics, are entirely unbothered by any scruples about becoming a nuisance, and have unquestionably become one, in practice if not in law, in a good many parts of North America other than Quebec. Like the Communists, the other present objects of the "burning hate" of that province, they were restrained during the war because of their violent opposition to military service, and indeed, to any other exercise of the civil power except such as suits their purposes.

B. K. SANDWELL

The recent judgment of the Supreme Court of Canada, which leaves the Jehovah's Witnesses completely free to distribute their circulars with impunity, has taken many people by surprise. The declaration that the freedom of religion must be equal for all is just if this refers to the fundamental freedom to worship and serve God within one's home or in churches and temples. The public worship of a cult should not be forbidden so long as it does not transgress upon the general populace.

Relations

The Bull was M. Duplessis who had sworn to ruin him (Charbonneau). . . . The slow-moving Cows were the group of reactionary bishops of that day, grouped under the confessionalist, nationalist, ruralist banner of Mgr. Courchesne, the archbishop of Rimouski, who saw himself as the saviour of the threatened Canadian Church. . . .

RENAUDE LAPOINTE

The widely-read magazine, *Time,* was impudent enough to suggest, mentioning the name of the Apostolic delegate, Mgr. Antoniutti, that Mgr. Charbonneau had been asked to change his attitude on the labour question. In a telegram addressed to the magazine and to the B.U.P. and P.C. press agencies, the Apostolic delegate "categorically denied that he had ever asked Mgr. Charbonneau *to draw back from his pro-labour stand* and that, on the contrary, he had always approved of and encouraged his very charitable attitude towards all the victims of war, strikes and social injustice."

Relations

The province of Quebec has just chosen the men who will hold public office for the next four years. . . . The wave of stupidity and immorality which Quebec has just witnessed cannot leave any lucid Catholic indifferent. Perhaps never before has the religious crisis which exists here been more clearly manifested. Never before have we been furnished a more striking proof of the dechristianization taking place among the masses.

GERARD DION & LOUIS O'NEILL

Part I

In the Beginning was...?

The Liberal Party had dominated Québec politics since 1897. Louis-Alexandre Taschereau was the Premier of Québec in 1935 and had been since 1920. He had succeeded Sir Lomer Gouin who had held the office from 1905 till the latter date. The provincial Conservative Party was in permanent disarray. Tenacious political memories persisted in associating it with the federal Conservative Party in power at the time of the hanging of Louis Riel, the First World War and the conscription issue. Arthur Sauvé had led the Tories in Québec from 1916 to 1929, and his successor was Camilien Houde. In 1933 a new Conservative leader was elected: Maurice Duplessis.

In Québec, as in most other areas of the world, the old order and the establishment were under attack during the Depression. The establishment appeared unwilling to or incapable of meeting new conditions. Québec was now more urban than rural as a result of a sustained period of industrialization from 1896 to 1929. The Depression had dampened prosperity and depressed spirits, but the Liberal government did not change.

Several ideologies, parties and personalities in Québec presented their solutions, and all viciously attacked the Liberal party of Taschereau, which was accused of too close association with English-Canadian and American trusts, as well as nepotism and corruption, not to mention inertia. The son of the former Premier of Québec, Paul Gouin, led a dissident Liberal group under the banner of *l'Action Libérale Nationale*. Its appeal was based on economic reform through nationalization, and political reform by means of self-conscious French Canadian nationalism, a form of crypto-separatism.

Another option available to Québec was that of Adrien Arcand. A thin, slight man, he scathingly and wittily attacked the old order in his paper, *Le Goglu*. The doctrines and policies of Mussolini and Hitler were his answers to hard times. Of more significance as a possible choice was the ideology of the Catholic Left, ably expounded by the young André Laurendeau. This ideology blended a sometimes strident, and sometimes moderate, French-Canadian nationalism with social and economic doctrines based on the *Rerum novarum* of the sometimes liberal pope, Leo XIII. Another ideology on the fringes was propounded by Paul Bouchard, the founder and editor of *La Nation*. He was first and foremost a separatist; his secondary theme was a variant of corporatism, a doctrine of social organization by professions and institutions. There was yet another force to be contended with: that of l'abbé Lionel Groulx, the most influential member of the group gathered about *l'Action Nationale*. Groulx was a recognized *nationaliste* leader and claimed to be apolitical. He conceived his role as that of a *nationaliste*, Catholic, and intellectual conscience prodding his people along the road of God's designs.

Political groups vied with political groups, personalities with personalities, ideologies with ideologies, and institutions with institutions. The past vied with the present, a present that was unacceptable to most people in Québec. The Duplessis phenomenon arose in this context.

Regardless of the ideological choices made, some viewed the basic problem as that of lack of leadership. *L'Action Nationale* held this idea. This stridently *nationaliste* publication had been founded by l'abbé Groulx in 1917 under the name of *Action française*, and it quickly became the champion of conservative Catholicism and French-Canadian nationalism. After the war, in 1922, it veered towards separatism. The review went through a crisis in the early 1930's as a result of its French homonym being placed under interdict. It changed its name, therefore, but not its ideology. The first reading reveals this personality cult as an ideal, and also indicates the stress the society placed on the concept of leadership as a means of solving the political, economic and social problems that plagued Québec and the world in the 1930's.

Duplessis was a *chef*, but of the Conservative Party of Québec. As such, he led his group against the entrenched Liberal Party headed by Louis-Alexandre Taschereau in the 1935 elections with but moderate success: 16 Conservatives were elected. Taschereau's more significant opposition came from *l'Action Libérale Nationale*. All opposition members in the Legislative Assembly of Québec were agreed upon the necessity of Taschereau's downfall, but they could not agree on who was to lead the opposition and take power after the Liberal government's fall. Andrew D. Savage's article in *Saturday Night*, a Liberal journal, recounts the jostling that led to the formation of *l'Union Nationale*, and Duplessis' ascendency in the party and in the province.

The *Electoral Catechism* was a Union Nationale propaganda document: it was a crude but effective attack on Taschereau, his cohorts and the Liberal Party, and those who refused to follow Duplessis' leadership. The title of this work was drawn from a book entitled *Catechisme Electoral*, published in 1851, and written by Antoine Gérin-Lajoie, a journalist, author and official translator of the Legislative Assembly of the Canadas in the pre-Confederation period. The original work was devoted to a consideration of political morality. As produced by the Union Nationale it fulfilled the same purpose albeit in a more partisan fashion.

The attacks on Taschereau led to his resignation, and in an election in 1936, the Duplessis forces elected 76 members as against the Liberals 14. The Duplessis era had begun.

Many viewed the new government as a reform movement. The *Montreal Gazette,* a newspaper with long-standing Conservative affiliations, illustrates the general attitude of the Anglophone press of Montreal: a good government co-operated with the interest of the establishment. Paul Bouchard, the editor of *La Nation,* also viewed Duplessis as a reformer and implied as well that the new leader was possibly the Messiah to lead the French Canadians to the promised land: separatism.

There were less charitable views, and it is to these misconceptions that Herbert F. Quinn, a specialist in Québec political history, addressed himself. The 1930's, particularly in Europe, were characterized by strong men. According to some, usually the English language press of Canada, the Québec electorate's choice in 1936 resembled all too closely the choice of the Germans, Italians, Portuguese and Spaniards. Quinn counters these views.

The economic crisis of the 1930's lessened towards the end of the decade; a new political crisis arose. Once again, as in the Great War, the French Canadians and Canada were faced by the double spectre of war and racism. These issues were further complicated by conflicts between Federal and provincial governments and between Mackenzie King's Liberals at Ottawa and Duplessis' Union Nationale in Québec.

Historians generally agree that Duplessis blundered badly in calling the disastrous election of 1939. The reasons for this defeat and the true significance of the election are considered by Frank Scott and 'Antonius'. (Professor Scott, until his retirement, taught law at McGill University and was at one time its Dean. He was an active member of the CCF, is a specialist in Canada constitutional law, and a well-known defender of civil rights). The interregnum in the Duplessis era lasted from his defeat until 1944. His and his party's views in the latter elections are given in the last selection. Duplessis must have struck sympathetic chords, for once he was returned to power, he remained there till he died in 1959.

"Un chef", *Action Nationale,* vol. V, no. 1, January 1935, pp. 3-4, (tr.)* Reprinted by permission of *Action Nationale.*

Un Chef?

In the topical speech which he delivered last June before the meeting of the Saint-Jean-Baptiste Society of Montreal, abbé Lionel Groulx ended a series of less than glorious statements by the following one, even more lamentable still: And we have no *chef*!

There is no doubt that from whatever point of view we consider it—social, economic, intellectual—our nation does not come out a very reassuring figure. A foreign yoke weighs on it and deprives it of that ethnic personality which attests a will to live, a will which is drawn from her own resources and generates pride.

If only we had a *chef,* a truly national *chef*! For a nation can free itself from any yoke, no matter how heavy or servile it is. It is sufficient if the nation desires to do so, and in order to so desire if it unites, and in order to unite if it groups itself about an ardent will.

An ardent will . . . that is to say, a *chef*!

"France needs a *chef*"! a French sociologist recently wrote, and he developed his thesis in a well-constructed book which he called by this phrase.

"French Canada needs a *chef*"! we might repeat in turn. A new day is dawning, a day of which we have little knowledge. A new order is being elaborated in which the theories to which we presently subscribe will perhaps appear out-of-date. Who will watch over our rights? Who will see to it that the basis of the pacts of union between the two races is respected? Who will be able to discern in the design of the future whether a home or a jail is being prepared for French thought?

A *chef*, a true *chef*, imbued with our traditions, strong in our faith, with a clear spirit, a firm will, and an ardent heart: this is what we imperatively need to survive. Our wish for the New Year is that Providence provides us with such a *chef*.

*The indication (tr.) means that the selection was translated by the editor, Cameron Nish.

"Maurice Duplessis", *Action Nationale,* vol. II, November 1933, pp. 171-174. (tr.) Reprinted by permission of *Action Nationale.*

In Joyful Battle

Bursting with energy, dynamic. His colouring, bearing and gait express a *joie de vivre,* a confidence in himself and in life. His step is agile, firm. Set in a strongly chiselled face, his eyes are dancing flames, cunning.

He loves joyful battle. Perhaps too much. One gets the feeling that he seeks out battles merely to satisfy his desire to attack, cross swords, and shoot arrows. Does he act out of conviction or is this merely a game? When he accosts a friend or opponent, the first contact is usually offensive. He teases, chaffs, and makes witty remarks that ordinarily strike home. Sometimes he wounds, but he is so outspoken and spirited that his victims take his blows gracefully.

A valuable frame of mind for the leader of the Opposition. In this never-ending duel, the mind becomes more acute, grows sharper, soon discovers the weak points of an argument or a situation and quickly turns them to best account.

On the floor of the House he is in his element. Few deputies attend as often as he. He is assiduous at every sitting, and sits only for the debate. Even when a deputy deals with an insignificant subject in a banal manner—which sometimes happens!—he listens with undivided attention, awaiting the right moment to intervene. A malicious smile foreshadowing the attack, the arrow always strikes home so as to produce its full effect on his opponent . . . and on the gallery.

There is seldom a day when he does not speak out several times. His words are awaited with impatience. Always cutting and unexpected, they add a lively note to the otherwise dull debates.

The deputy from Three Rivers has introduced into parliamentary debates a polemical tone marked by spirit, dignity and gentility. Although he can be biting when the opportunity arises, he always stays within certain bounds. He prides himself on "never hitting an opponent below the belt." He is reluctant to use certain weapons, a restraint which some of his less scrupulous supporters hold against him.

Maurice Duplessis is by no means a great public orator. He speaks without research and with surprisingly careless form and pronunciation. People listen to him attentively because he is clear, precise, and goes straight to the heart of a matter without shilly-shallying. He seeks to convince less by eloquence than by reason. His oratorical style is subdued. He seldom gestures. When he argues closely, a pointed index finger punctuates his reasoning. When he wants to flash wit or to tease wickedly, he holds his hands behind his back and throws forward his chest with an air of confident defiance.

But it is above all as an organizer that he is a past master. He knows men and his intuition correctly tells him where he should direct his efforts. Prudent and self-controlled, he leaves nothing to chance, for he knows that pure chance is not a stable sign of success.

Until now Duplessis has, in particular, owed his success to his use of those qualities which are secondary to statesmen: the ability to organize, an ease of elocution, versatility, a keen sense of judgment, a legal bent acquired through family tradition and his personal experience as a lawyer. He has not shown himself to be sufficiently cultured, nor to have that breadth of vision which would enable him to consider a problem in every dimension, nor, perhaps, to possess the inner flame or devotion of a prophet. This explains why he has not yet been able to draw up a strictly original program, nor to devote his name and talent to any great national question.

But it would be unwise to draw conclusions too quickly. Duplessis is young. He is game, ambitious, determined. His responsibilities as a party leader are already giving a different colour to his attitudes. His past augurs well of the future.

His friends reproach him for too often "having his own way." This is the quality of a *chef*: provided he does not push it too far and try to settle everything without any advice whatsoever. Until now the policy which the young *chef* of the opposition has followed has proved effective. . . . There is too much worry and disgust in the air for present problems to be solved within the old frameworks and by the old means.

The people ardently desire a *chef* who will bring about a new order. Can Maurice Duplessis be that *chef*? Does he want to be?

Andrew D. Savage, "No Holds Are Barred in Quebec Political Fight", *Saturday Night,* vol. 54, no. 11, January 14, 1939, p. 2.

The Union Nationale: Unholy Alliance

Quebec politics are as exciting as an Oppenheim adventure story. There are intrigues, plots and counterplots, double-crossings, threats of disclosures of incredible corruptions, and secret and unholy alliances designed to explode some political bombshell. Yet nothing ever happens. At times the continuous deluge of malign political gossip is due to Gallic imagination, and at other times to Gallic realism which sees behind each political move a sinister cause. So involved are the sudden swerves and alliances in the Quebec political scene that few Anglo-Saxons have the time or the mental agility to follow the situation. They shrug their shoulders and say: "Oh, the French!" . . .

Maurice Duplessis . . . was a Conservative, and only came to power by allying his party with l'Action Nationale. This was an attempt to combine God and Mammon, for l'Action Nationale is anything but conservative, comprising as it does all the ginger boys of the Province. They hate the English, they hate the power barons, they hate the corporations, and above all they hate the boys behind the scenes in the provincial Liberal party. These last, so they feel, sold the simple, godly French-Canadian into the bondage of a group of cursed English highwaymen, generically referred to as "les trustards."

L'Action Nationale is typical of a whole series of French-Canadian political movements all of which start off with violent verbal explosions and ultimately come to naught. Like firecrackers, Quebec politics are designed to provide more noise and fun than force.

Paul Gouin, son of the late Sir Lomer Gouin, heads l'Action Nationale. The inspiration of many of its wilder ideas is one Abbé Groulx whose cloth adds weight to his ideas. Nevertheless, many of his views are not in accord with those which obtain in the Cardinal's palace at Quebec.

Behind Gouin are lined up all the hot-heads of the Province. They include many of the younger French-Canadians, those equipped with years of training but who can't find jobs; those who want to seize Sir Herbert Holt's power plants; those who dream of "Laurentia," the new French and Catholic republic on the shores of the noble St. Lawrence; those who would restrict the teaching of English in the schools; and those who want no truck nor trade with the English.

Back of l'Action Nationale exists a very secret organization known as the Société Jacques Cartier, devoted to the foregoing aims. But it is so secret that it has not much force. . . .

When Duplessis came into power, he proceeded to fall out with Paul Gouin. Of course most of the l'Action Nationale members stuck with the leader of the Union Nationale. And why not? A member must not lose his patronage rights.

The Liberals claim that Duplessis has since won by-elections only because the French-Canadians realize that it is useless to elect a member to the Opposition benches. He can spend no government largesse in the constituency. . . .

Politically however, l'Action Nationale has a great nuisance value. Time and again it is said that Paul Gouin has been approached by the Liberals and by the political groups anxious to obtain his support. But it is said that l'Action Nationale keeps its price too high.

In the meantime, Duplessis feels he is sitting pretty. There is dissension amongst the nationalistic ginger boys, and there is dissension in the provincial Liberal camp. Duplessis still has a huge majority in the House, but he continues to lose friends. Not only did he break with Gouin, but he fired two of his ministers, one of whom, in true Quebec style, refused to resign. This rather put it up to Maurice Duplessis, because a minister of the Crown cannot be fired like an office boy. The difficulty was, however, overcome in a proper statesmanlike and constitutional manner. Mr. Duplessis himself resigned. This threw all the cabinet out of a job, at any rate for an hour or two. Immediately the Lieutenant-Governor called on Mr. Duplessis to form a new cabinet. This he did, omitting to mention the name of the recalcitrant Mr. Leduc. It sounds like comic opera; it is comic opera.

French Catholics say that Duplessis takes all his orders directly from the Church. And in Quebec it does not matter what the English think; their views have no political weight. In French circles it is now openly stated that the Church never had more influence with the Government, and less with the people of the Province.

The truth of the matter is that Duplessis is first and foremost a good Catholic, hence there exists a *rapport* between his point of view and that of the clergy. . . .

While the French Canadian "city feller" now views Duplessis with some degree of suspicion, he seems to be liked in the back parishes. And it is the voters of St. Polycarpe-de-Trois-Pistoles and St. Edwidge-de-Ham who control the Legislative Assembly. Just how long Duplessis will be able to hold the back concessions depends on the activities of the Liberal party which, as far as provincial politics are concerned, is strangely weak. . . .

The Duplessis government came into power breathing fire and brimstone against the big interests. And nothing happened. In fact it is now alleged that he is hand in glove with the fat boys of the Province, the very "trustards" who wrecked Taschereau. His opponents claim that whenever a scent leading to a trustard really becomes hot, Duplessis calls off the bloodhounds.

One of the pleasing features of Mr. Duplessis is that even his hottest opponents pay high tribute to his personal honesty. He is an upright man. Naturally, the Liberals allege that the iniquities which his government is presently perpetrating outrun anything which the Taschereau régime achieved even in its palmiest, or rather its palmoiliest, days. But it is really impossible to believe that anything could equal, let alone surpass, in this regard the Government which Duplessis overthrew.

Truth to tell, Duplessis has carried a terrific burden. His followers came into power after watching their opponents wallow in the public trough for forty long years, and were they all hungry for the spoils! True, Duplessis has let the Abitibi power project job on a cost-plus basis without asking for tenders. But with all the pressure on the man, it is strange that his opponents have not had more to squawk about.

If Duplessis passes ultimately into a complete and final eclipse, it will be due to a combination of several factors. First there is his belief that he can turn the clock back—or perhaps forward—by padlocking ideas; second, the Liberals might pull a real leader out of the bag; and third, the French-Canadian likes tradition, and the Liberals can continue to cash in on the tradition of Laurier, the tradition of being opposed to conscription, and the tradition of being a party of grands seigneurs.

Le Catechisme des électeurs, d'après l'ouvrage de A. Gérin-Lajoie, (Montréal, J. B. Thivierge & Fils, 1936), pp. 26-29, 32-34, 41, 73-80. (tr.)

Electoral Catechism

ON THE POWERS OF MONEY

31.—Who are the money powers?

—They are certain directors of banks, finance companies, large industries and big business who conspire in order to advance, defend and protect their own interests at the expense of the public interest.

32.—How do the money powers manage to dominate the government of the province?

—They do so, above all, by taking ministers, deputy-ministers, and the relatives of ministers into their businesses. . . .

35.—Do the ministers of Quebec model themselves after the leading politicians of the world who, wishing to avoid a conflict between their private interests and the public interest, refuse to become directors of large companies?

—Apparently not, inasmuch as Mr. Taschereau, for example, Mr. Godbout's master, is a director of Barclay's Bank, even though he is not a banker; he is a director of Sun Life, the Metropolitan Life, and the North American Life, even though he is not an insurance dealer; he is a director of the Crédit Foncier, even though he does not loan money on real estate; moreover, he is a director of eight other companies. . . .

ON THE GREAT REMEDY TO THIS GREAT EVIL

54.—How then can we get rid of both the money powers, the trusts, and their influence, and the politicians who are their slaves?

—The only way to get rid of both the money powers, the trusts, and their influence, and the politicians who are the slaves is to overthrow the Taschereau-Godbout Regime.

55.—*How can the Taschereau-Godbout Regime be overthrown?*

—By voting in this provincial election for the candidates of the Union Nationale which groups all the free liberals, the free conservatives, all the independents and all the true patriots of the province in a popular party similar to the party which brought Mercier to power long ago. . . .

ON THE "FAMILY COMPACT"

108.—What do we call that behaviour which consists in protecting one's own in an extravagant and exaggerated fashion after one has received a public mandate?

—According to common sense and the dictionary, we call this nepotism . . . or in our simple and vivid popular tongue: feathering one's own nest.

109.—Are there, by any chance, any relatives, by blood or by marriage, of the Honourable Alexandre Taschereau who live out of the nest?

—Not counting women, there are about forty individuals, relatives . . . of Mr. Taschereau, who live directly or indirectly out of the nest or off of the nest. Of course, this is purely coincidental!

110.—How long have the Taschereaus lived at the public's expense?

—Since 1736.

111.—Could you name a few of the relatives . . . of Mr. Godbout's leader who earn their bread and their livelihood from the administration, the judiciary, or positions more or less tributary to government?

1—Louis-Alexandre Taschereau, until recently the Prime Minister and President of the Council: $16,500 per year—$14,000 as Prime Minister and $2,500 as the deputy for Montmorency. (This does not include what he draws from the "trusts").

2—Antoine Taschereau, Alexandre's brother, the too-expert accountant of the Legislative Assembly and the dismissed secretary of the Quebec School Commission: $6,500 per year. Without taking into account the interest on public funds entrusted to him, which he regularly puts into his own pocket.

3—Robert Taschereau, Alexandre's son: until recently, $2,500 per year as the deputy for Bellechasse, and about $10,000 per year as a lawyer for companies needing the favours and privileges of government.

4—Paul Taschereau, Alexandre's son: about $10,000 as a lawyer for several companies which are friends of the government, and especially for Quebec Power, the Canadian Bank of Commerce, *et al.*

5—Charles-Edmond Taschereau, Alexandre's brother, public notary and notary for several government departments: about $10,000 per year from companies needing the favours of government . . . Ex-secretary of the Municipal Bonds Corporations, which ended in bankruptcy and disaster. . . .

8—André Taschereau, Alexandre's nephew, lawyer in the law firm of Saint-Laurent, Devlin Gagné, . . . : numerous honorariums for professional services; his name constantly crops up in the budget. . . .

17—C.-E. de Montarville Taschereau, the Prime Minister's cousin, employee of the Department of National Defence: about $3,000 per year. . . .

21.—R.-A. Benoît, Alexandre's nephew, secretary of the Legislative Council: $6,000 per year. . . .

27—J.-Hughes Fortier, Alexandre's cousin, Chief Justice of the Court of Sessions. . . .

36—Paul Lemieux, Edmond Taschereau's nephew, on the Quebec Liquor Commission: about $1,500 per year. . . .

And this list is not complete, for we have only cited the male relatives . . . of Mr. Godbout's leader.

Montreal Gazette, Monday, July 13, 1936.

The Union Nationale: Holy Alliance

Programme of the Union Nationale for the forthcoming provincial elections as outlined yesterday afternoon by Maurice Duplessis, K.C., at Baie du Febvre, Yamaska County:

1—An honest election law with provision that all political parties shall make known the full list of slush fund subscribers.

2—A new law for contested elections, retroactive in effect.

3—Provincial farmers' credit with money at not more than 4 per cent., and, if today's conditions hold, not over 3 per cent.

4—A stop to spoon-fed agriculture —abolition of distribution of farmers' bonuses with political partizanship.

5—Support for "professional association" to place agriculture above political skullduggery.

6—A real colonization programme; classification of colonist lands and separation from forest domains; an end to obstacles to land settlement by the "big lumber trusts."

7—Establishment of true representative Government and an end to government by lawyers.

8—Reform of the Legislative Council to make of it an Economic Council.

9—Full liberty in education; preeminence of the religious authorities to be recognized.

10—Just spread of taxation in the Province of Quebec with experts to advise Government on changes to be made.

11—Economy; abolition of superfluous commissions; retrenchment by close watch on expenditures, substitution of open tenders for closed tenders for Government supplies, etc.

12—No added taxation to meet the party's agricultural programme which would be financed out of savings on present operations.

13—Abolition of the post of "commercial agent" for Quebec in London.

14—Better distribution of ministries in the Cabinet.

15—Denunciation and jailing of canaille financiers exploiting public misery.

16—Handcuffs on the electricity trust.

17—Rural electrification and reasonable hydro rates for the farmer.

18—No purchase of Government supplies from the coal trust or the hydro trust.

19—Proper guarantees for honest property and an end to usury.

20—Honest company laws; no stock manipulations or watering.

21—Preservation of natural wealth for the people of today and for future generations.

22—Changes in the Workmen's Compensation Act, with the injured man having the right to choose his own doctor.

23—Minimum wage laws for workers.

24—Continuation "to the end" of the investigation into Government departments started by the Public Accounts Committee of the Legislative Assembly with Mr. Duplessis himself guiding the probe.

Paul Bouchard, "Victoire de l'Union Nationale", *La Nation,* (Québec), première année no. 28, 20 août, 1936. (tr.)

First Step Towards Separatism

"The Union Nationale's victory marks, for the first time in the history of our province, the complete dissociation of provincial parties from federal parties. . . . I will even go as far as to say that, if Duplessis keeps his promise to implement the Action Nationale program, provincial policies will soon come into such conflict with the federal government that the Union Nationale will either lead us straight to separatism, to the creation of a free French State in America, or Duplessis in turn will fall from power. Let all enthusiasts of the Union Nationale who believe in its leaders and in the curative virtues of its political program not forget the following: all obstacles to our emancipation will come from the federal government. The emancipation of the French Canadians is impossible within the framework of Confederation, and it is the Union Nationale whose political destiny it is to give us a practical and irrevocable demonstration of this fact. I thus salute its victory as the first step towards a free French State, even though this is not the intention of its leader, who is rather hostile to this idea, nor an article of its program.

. . . Without doubt, we will witness a new edition of the pan-Canadian adventure of 1911 and we will see several former colonial *bleus* and illusionists of the old generation ask Ottawa to apply the letter and the spirit of Confederation in its entirety. They may perhaps keep the French Canadian nation to this federal error for another ten years and will delay accordingly the fulfilment of its historic destiny. In the long run, the result of these vain efforts will still be secession.

. . . If we are to get out of the provincial and federal marasmus, there is only one possible outcome: secession. This is what the Union Nationale is leading us to! Perhaps its leaders do not entirely realize this, but they will continue to be the puppets of events. . . .

Towards all and against all, we remain separatists.

H. F. Quinn, "The Bogey of Fascism in Quebec", *Dalhousie Review*, vol. 28, October 1938, pp 301-308. Reprinted by permission of the Author and *The Dalhousie Review.*

Bogey or Fascism?

It is is a common belief in many sections of Canada and the United States that the Province of Quebec is advancing rapidly along the road to Fascism, and is only awaiting the appearance of a *Führer* who will set up a totalitarian dictatorship on the banks of the St. Lawrence, dissolve all political parties, crush the labour unions, regiment industry, liquidate all Communists, Socialists and Liberals, and establish a Corporative State, all with the approval if not the actual support of the Roman Catholic hierarchy in the province. . . .

It is true that the most significant feature of Quebec politics to-day is the re-birth of French-Canadian Nationalism, which has appeared at different intervals in the past with varying intensity, and which is characterized by an emphasis upon the strengthening of the bonds of French-Canadian culture, a resistance to Americanization, and a policy of Quebec for the French-Canadians. This policy, be it noted, does not necessarily imply Separatism, and secession from the Dominion of Canada, much less the setting up of a Fascist State in Quebec, for it must be remembered that Quebec Nationalism was an important factor in the political life of the Dominion long before Fascism was ever heard of. It does imply a tendency to resist all attempts upon the part of the federal government at Ottawa to extend its influence over provincial affairs, and a desire on the part of the French-Canadian to participate to a greater extent in the economic development of the province, which up to the present time has been largely due to American and English capital. . . .

Dissatisfaction with existing economic conditions, and particularly the predominant part played by the English-speaking section of the population in the economic life of the province, together with the corruption prevalent under the existing régime, resulted in a realignment of political forces in the Fall of 1935, and the formation of a so-called National Union Party headed by M. Maurice Duplessis, and made up of both Conservatives and dissident Liberals headed by M. Paul Gouin. The chief purpose of the National Union Party was the overthrow of the Taschereau Government, at whose door all the ills of the province were laid. It was accused of surrendering to the forces of the English financiers, and selling the French-Canadian's birthright for a mess of pottage.

The formation of the National Union Party, however, was only one aspect of the Nationalist movement in Quebec, although it was by far the most important one. More or less coinciding with the appearance of this group, there sprang into existence many smaller intensely Nationalistic movements, such as *La Jeunesse Nationale, Le Jeune Canada, La Nation de Quebec. . . .*

Moreover, the aims of these organizations cannot be termed Fascistic in the strict sense of the word. The basic principles of all these groups are pretty much the same, although there is sometimes a difference of emphasis on certain points. In general, however, their programmes are characterized by anti-Semitism, and a certain amount of anti-English feeling; an intense Nationalism which sometimes expresses itself in what is known as Separatism, i.e., the promotion of a separate French-Canadian State on the banks of the St. Lawrence; a demand for the reform of Capitalism and the curbing of Communism; and advocacy of a system of Christian Corporatism as the ideal form of social organization. There is no demand for the setting up of a totalitarian dictatorship on the German or Italian model.

The only organization in the Province of Quebec which can be termed Fascist is the National Christian Social Party whose *Führer* is M. Adrien Arcand. This avowedly Fascist organization publishes its own monthly paper, *Le Fasciste Canadien,* is violently anti-Semitic, repudiates democracy and advocates authoritarian principles in politics, makes war on Communism, Socialism and Liberalism, attacks "Finance Capitalism", and has as its ultimate goal the establishment in Canada of a totalitarian Corporative State on the German and Italian models. . . .

The main points in the programme of the new group were the greater participation of the French-Canadian in the economic development of the province, a greater emphasis upon the development of a distinctive French-Canadian culture, and the strengthening of the bonds of race and religion; a thorough investigation into the prevailing system of political patronage, and the elimination of corruption in public affairs; the curbing of the trusts and the passing of legislation that would facilitate the municipalization of electricity; legislation guaranteeing fair wages and better working conditions for employees in industry, and the further development of the prevailing Collective Labour Agreement Extension Act in the direction of the corporative organization of society as laid down by Pope Pius XI in his encyclical *Quadragesimo Anno.*

Although the National Union Party came to power riding on the crest of the wave of Nationalism, and although it had gained many adherents by capitalizing on the prevalent anti-trust sentiment, which was to a very large extent anti-English sentiment, nevertheless, when once in power M. Duplessis lost no time in repudiating any desire on his part for the secession of the province from the Dominion of Canada, and went out of his way to reassure the English-speaking people that his government was impelled by no merely anti-English or anti-Capitalistic bias, but wished to secure for the French-Canadian his proper share in the economic development of the province.

It is a cardinal principle in M. Duplessis's political philosophy that if the people of the Province of Quebec are to achieve material prosperity, and Quebec is to take its place alongside Ontario as one of the chief industrial provinces of Canada, there must be harmony in the relations between Capital and Labour. As a means of eliminating industrial strife, and at the same time advancing the cause of social justice, the Duplessis government strongly advocates the principles of Corporatism.

There is in the Province of Quebec to-day a strong and rapidly growing body of opinion which inclines towards the Corporative concept of society. Corporatism finds its adherents not only amongst the members of the present government, but also amongst the smaller Nationalistic groups and particularly amongst the Roman Catholic clergy. . . .

It is difficult to understand Quebec politics unless one realizes the great part played in them by the fear of Communism, which is one of the greatest bogies of the present government and a prime factor in its policy. . . .

Despite all this, to tag M. Duplessis as a Fascist or the advocate of a Fascist State is absurd. Duplessis is no potential Hitler or Mussolini aspiring to dictatorship, but on the other hand is a typical politician of the old school of party politics and parliamentary government. There is no anti-Semitism, racialism, totalitarianism or anti-democratic tendency in the policy of the present government. Strikes are not forbidden; labour unions, whether Catholic or international, have retained their autonomy; wages under the Duplessis régime have been raised rather than lowered; business is not being regimented, the freedom of the press has not been violated, the right to criticize freely the policy and activities of the government has not been curtailed, and indeed attacks upon the government by its political opponents are more violent and vociferous than ever. The by-elections which have been held since the new government came into power have been conspicuously free from any taint of corruption or coercion. The very organizations which are so loud in their denunciation of the suppression of free speech in Quebec, such as the Civil Liberties Union and the C. C. F. Party, are continually holding meetings and rallies, and discussing openly the loss of the freedom which they are exercising. . . .

Another widespread mistake is the tendency to hold the Roman Catholic Church in Quebec accountable for many things which are not the result of Catholic teachings, but are due to the traditions and racial characteristics of the French-Canadian, and the peculiarities of his culture. In this respect it is interesting to note the hostility in the province towards the proposal of female suffrage. Now the Roman Catholic Church has never declared against the principle of female suffrage, and has never made it an article of faith that women must not participate in politics, and it is obvious that the attitude towards this question in Quebec is prompted by racial rather than religious principles. For while it is true that women are denied the right to vote in Catholic Quebec, it is equally true that this right is denied them in anti-clerical France.

F. R. Scott, "The Real Vote in Quebec", *Canadian Forum,* vol. XIX, no. 227, December 1939, pp. 270-271. Reprinted by permission of the Author.

Godbout Becomes God

Now that the figures of the total vote cast in the Quebec elections are available, it is possible to form a fairly reliable estimate of what happened in that province on October 25th. The imperialist press in Canada, as was to be expected, immediately interpreted the Liberal victory as proof that the people of Quebec were solidly behind Canada's war effort. The Winnipeg Free Press, the Globe and Mail of Toronto, and the Montreal Star showed the unity of their war attitude by the similarity of their misinterpretations. Mr. Grant Dexter of the Free Press summarized the situation in this way: "Quebec was offered two choices, to unite Canada in unlimited voluntary participation in the war, or to withdraw from the war and to resist the war effort of Canada; she chose the first." The Globe and Mail almost seemed to think that the vote justified the introduction of conscription. One and all were as eager and ready to read war approval into the election results as any of the newspapers in England.

This kind of wishful thinking is quite erroneous, and highly dangerous to the very national unity it pretends to understand. The press in English Canada should cease misinterpreting Quebec in this way and trying to promote war policies based on a false assumption; or else another rift may be created in the future even greater than any which has existed in the past. There are certain very definite advantages for Canadian unity which may result from the fall of Duplessis; to try to exploit the situation for purely imperialist ends is to show an ignorance of Quebec and a disregard for the future welfare of this country.

The first requisite to an understanding of Quebec's choice is to look at the vote. Canadian Press returns for 84 out of 86 constituencies show the following figures:

Party	1939	%	1936	%
Liberal	287,673	52.73	226,006	40.37
Union Nationale	217,460	39.86	315,418	56.33
A.L.N. (Gouin)	24,893	4.57	———	———
Others	15,573	2.84	18,457	3.30
Total	545,599		559,881	

In other words, the Liberals defeated all other parties by some 30,000 votes only, Duplessis and Gouin between them obtained 44.43% of the votes—and Gouin was more anti-war than Duplessis. Even assuming, therefore, that all who voted Liberal did so because they wanted active participation in the war (which is fantastic), it still remains true that the great Liberal majority in favour of Mr. Grant Dexter's "unlimited voluntary participation" amounts to about 8%. There is obviously a great deal of anti-war feeling in the province of Quebec today, no matter what interpretation is placed upon the election result. To ignore it is to overlook a factor of continuing importance.

The next step that must be taken to

understand the situation is to weigh the motives that led the voters to support Mr. Godbout and the Liberals. This is admittedly a difficult task, since the element of conjecture cannot be eliminated. Certain broad issues, however, are clear. Quebec was not offered the choice of "withdrawing from the war" by anyone. There was no possibility of any such action, and the ordinary man on the farms and in the street had sense enough to know it. Equally was it true that there was no party in Quebec which made active participation in the war a principal part of its program. Quebec did not vote for war. Certain independent Conservatives in English speaking constituencies did run as imperialists, and they lost their deposits. A number of Liberals in the same constituencies were equally pro-war and were elected, but in the French districts the Liberals were anti-conscription rather than pro-war. The Liberal vote as a whole, in so far as it expressed any idea at all in regard to the war, was primarily an anti-conscription vote. This is why Mr. Lapointe's intervention was so supremely important. Once he had announced, in his opening speech, that in the event of a Duplessis victory he would resign with all his French colleagues in the Federal Cabinet, it became clear that a vote for Mr. Duplessis would be more likely to bring on conscription than retard it. For Mr. Lapointe was opposed to conscription, and if he left the Cabinet was it not likely that the crisis would be met by the formation of a national government, as in 1917, for the express purpose of overriding French opposition? Le Canada, the official Liberal paper, stressed this argument on more than one occasion; on the morning of the election its chief headline read: "Votre vote renforcira la position que nous avons prise contre la conscription, declare M. Cardin." Quebec preferred to accept the fact of our present commitment to the war, which it could not change in any way, with the repeated promises that all enlistment would remain voluntary, rather than run the risk of having at Ottawa a far more pro-war government managed by imperialists.

But the war issue was only one of the issues in the election, and it is doubtful whether it was even the main issue. No matter how much the war might be introduced, the electors knew well enough that they were choosing a provincial administration to look after provincial affairs. Mr. Duplessis had much to answer for. His financial dealings, which had more than doubled the provincial debt in three years, left him wide open to attack, and Mr. Godbout centred his campaign round the financial question. It was not difficult to convince the electorate that the war issue had been dragged in as a blind to cover up the serious crisis in the treasury department, and further that if Mr. Duplessis were elected he would receive no money from Ottawa and hence would be forced to resort to high taxation. A large part of the Liberal vote can be attributed to this argument alone. Then much of the labour legislation of the Union Nationale, particularly such things as rendering unincorporated trades-unions liable in damages and collective agreements liable to alteration by government decree, were distasteful to labour generally. The farmers had been better treated by Mr. Duplessis and supported him more loyally, but even here his promises had outreached his achievements. Mr. Godbout, also, is a good agriculturist. Purely provincial motives of this kind must have determined the votes of a great proportion of the electorate. If Mr. Duplessis had been genuinely concerned to protect the autonomy of Quebec, he could have used his large majority and his two more years of power at once, instead of calling an election.

In short, the extreme interpretations that followed the announcement of the election results were decidedly misplaced. The people of Quebec, while willing to support the defence of their shores, no more like the idea of Canada taking part in European wars today than they did six months ago. But they are a sensible people, and the fact that a vote for Duplessis would not take Canada out of the war was plain to everyone. As the popular vote showed, they altered their political alignments very little. So long as Quebec retains the present electoral system, without proportional representation or the alternative vote, changes of government will not give a true picture of the movement of public opinion. Particularly erroneous was a remark in the Winnipeg Free Press editorial of October 27th to the effect that "The present situation in Quebec is in happy contrast to that in the last war." Actually the contrast is all the other way. In 1914 Canada's participation evoked far less protest than has been seen already in this war. This time there has been no statement approving the war issued by the hierarchy in Quebec, as was done in the pastoral letter issued to the dioceses of Quebec, Montreal and Ottawa on October 22nd, 1914. This time a petition signed by many thousand people was presented to Parliament, opposing participation, and rejected because of its form; this did not occur in 1914. And this time one leading French Canadian politician thought he could secure another term of office by capitalising on the anti-war sentiment; had his domestic record been better, he would probably have succeeded. It is more true today than it was in 1914 that participation in overseas war strains our national unity. Any future attempt to introduce conscription would make that fact abundantly clear.

Duplessis became a Communist
Communists became pro-Hitler
Westmount became liberal
Godbout became God

This analysis of what occurred in Quebec last October still leaves it possible to interpret the vote as being favourable to the concept of national unity, so long as that term is not identified with unlimited participation. Unity and war participation have no necessary connection. A man may favour national unity, and yet believe this war not to be in Canada's interests. Mr. Duplessis had pushed too far his idea of provincial autonomy. The vote at least showed that this appeal can be overdone. Non-co-operation from Quebec in such things as unemployment insurance and other matters of national importance has simply meant that the working classes do not get as much protection as they otherwise might get. Separatism means a lower standard of living for Quebec, and probably many people on relief or near it perceive the fact. The bogey of assimilation has served its turn for a while, and it looks as though appeals to such false fears are not as powerful as we have thought. All this is to the good. There is a real opportunity for increased co-operation from the new administration in the solution of national domestic problems, particularly in the matters that will be dealt with in the report of the Sirois Commission on Dominion-Provincial relations. Anyone who endangers this by trying to capitalize on the Quebec vote for imperialist reasons is undermining Canadian unity.

Antonius, "The Quebec Election", *Saturday Night,* vol. 55, no. 8, December 23, 1939, p. 5. Reprinted by permission of *Saturday Night.*

Antonius Comments

The importance of the issues involved alone leads me to offer some criticism of your laudatory Front Page reference to Professor F. R. Scott's recent article in the *Canadian Forum.*

Far from giving a correct picture of the inferences which may be drawn from the results of the recent provincial election in Quebec, Professor Scott's statements seem to me to present an entirely biased and unfair view.

I can pin this charge down directly by pointing out that, in a labored attempt to prove that the attitude of the French-Canadian people in the present war is not as favorable to participation as that which existed in 1914, Professor Scott goes so far as to suggest that the Church to which the great majority of our French-Canadian citizens belong has not taken as definite a position in participation in this War as was the case 25 years ago. Since Professor Scott chooses to offer the opinions of the Church—as he interprets them, I may—although I regret the tendency of non-Roman Catholics, like Professor Scott and myself, to comment on the internal affairs of a communion to which we do not belong—present the fact that His Eminence the Cardinal Archbishop of Quebec, in a recent speech at Washington, D.C., is quoted in the press as having said specifically that the vote of Quebec is to be interpreted as one in favor of Canadian national unity.

It was my privilege to live in the Province of Quebec throughout the War of 1914 to 1918, and to watch, from a very favored standpoint, the development of the anti-war sentiment which became general here among many of our French-speaking citizens towards the close of the struggle. I can testify, from personal knowledge, that, as Professor Scott points out, the French-speaking Canadians accepted the necessity of Canadian participation in the war with equanimity, and, in the case of a great many of them, with ardent expressions of loyalty to the British Crown. They were met with an attitude, on the part of the military authorities of the Dominion, which can only be described as insolent. It was made quite clear that no concession was to be made to the fact that, to a large percentage of the people of our province, the French language is the only possible vehicle of instruction. No attempt was made in the early days of the war to recruit definitely French-Canadian units. No publicity was given to the fact that thousands of French-Canadians enlisted in the Canadian Expeditionary Force. When a special recruiting effort in this province became necessary, the officer placed in charge of this was an English-speaking minister of a Protestant denomination. Finally, in response to a wave of ignorant denunciation of the French-Canadian race, conscription was adopted in an election marked by all the bitterness which could be aroused on the side of the conscriptionists; the law providing for this was then set at naught with the open knowledge of the authorities at Ottawa; it became generally known that political influence and even bribery could be used to obtain exemption; and, in the end, when public opinion in the rest of the country became even more heated, the conscription law was enforced with an indiscriminate brutality, which left an almost indelible mark on the minds of the rural population in particular.

At all times, the appeal to the French-Canadian was to fight for Britain, or for France.

All of this clumsy handling of a delicate situation was applied to a population at that time comparatively indifferent to world affairs, and, with the exception of a small number of intellectuals, uninformed as to the issues at stake. In contrast, the present war was no surprise to the French-Canadian people. The increased interest in international affairs—specially stimulated by the general use of the radio—had made them far more familiar with the situation in Europe. The issue was definitely known to be one, not between rival imperialisms, but between oppression and liberty. A discussion of the international situation had long been conducted in Canada with very definite relation to the place which Canada, as a nation, must play in the struggle. When war broke out, the question of Canadian participation was explicitly discussed, not on a basis of our duty to the British Empire, nor of the racial connection between a group of Canadians and a foreign country, but as a case in which the people of a free nation had a free choice. From the moment that our participation in the war became obviously inevitable, the references to French Canada in the press of the rest of the country, and in general discussion among the English-speaking Canadians in Quebec, were at all times friendly and optimistic. There was a general appreciation expressed of the special conditions which would affect French-Canadian opinion. Every effort was made to see that those French-Canadians who wished to serve in the armed forces were given an opportunity to do so in circumstances which would prevent any friction. From the first it was understood that special French-Canadian units would be enlisted, and the striking fact that the first infantry unit in Canada to recruit an active service battalion to strength was the Regiment de Maisonneuve was given marked attention in the press of all Canada.

As a result, the French-speaking people of Canada have not, at any time, shown anything but a truly Canadian attitude. They have shown every intention of doing their full share in a war in which their country is engaged as a nation.

That some of them—a considerable percentage, if Professor Scott desires to stress this fact—are dubious of the wisdom of Canadian participation on a large scale is not to be denied. It could scarcely be otherwise. Some of our more vociferous English-Canadian nationalists have been very much of this opinion. For years before the outbreak of the present war many of the younger professors in our universities were notable for utterances which could only be interpreted as protesting against any idea of Canadian participation on the side of Britain and France in war. At least one of our younger English-speaking Senators also took this stand. In fairness, it is to be admitted that many of these individuals have at least ceased their propaganda, and some of them have openly recanted. Only recently, seventy-five ministers of the United Church passed a resolution against Canadian participation in the war. It is not surprising that there is an element among the French Canadians who hold similar opinions. However, to the knowledge of all who are in daily contact with them, the French-Canadian people have shown a unanimity in their desire to maintain a united national policy which is very striking.

Professor Scott goes to great mathematical trouble to prove that the popular vote in the late election was not overwhelmingly for the war. He even includes, among those who must be regarded as not necessarily for the war, the numbers of the voters for candidates in Montreal and its suburbs who took their stand on a platform of straight Conservatism—objecting to the election of Liberal members at Quebec, on the ground that they were not sufficiently imperialist.

Professor Scott is quite right in saying that not every vote cast *against* the Duplessis Government was so cast as a result of consideration of the war issue. I can assure him that not every vote *for* the Duplessis Government was cast against participation in the war. It was totally impossible to convince the electors of Sherbrooke that Lt.-Col. the Hon. J. S. Bourque—a distinguished French-Canadian soldier—was against participation in the war, merely because he supported the Duplessis Government, or the electors of Brome that the Hon. Jonathan Robinson—an English-speaking Canadian of a well-known Loyalist family—wished Canada to withdraw from the Empire. I quote these cases to indicate the fallacy of Professor Scott's approach to the question.

In the last analysis, I am driven to the conclusion that all that Professor Scott is attempting to do is to justify his own stand in his book "Canada Today." In that volume, he argued that Canadian unity would not stand the shock of a declaration of war. It has done so, and the Quebec election was the outstanding demonstration of his error of judgment. For my part I find it extremely regrettable that, in order to justify an erroneous position, Professor Scott should now undertake to carry on and accentuate his campaign of incorrect statements as to the French-Canadian attitude.

"Duplessis Assails Government Here", *Montreal Gazette,* September 23, 1942.

Quebec is Loyal Enough

Buckingham, Que., September 22—Chilly atmospheric conditions did not dampen the enthusiasm of the citizens of the county of Papineau from turning out this evening at an open air meeting in the college yard to hear Maurice Duplessis, National Union leader and his lieutenants of this western part of the province.

Mr. Duplessis was given a very warm greeting.

When he had come into power in 1936, he declared, it was found the previous Government had left debts of 48 millions unpaid, on which high rates of interest were being paid, and the first task of the new Government had been to borrow 51 millions at a rate of interest lower than ever before. The National Union Government had re-established the farmers despite the claim of Mr. Godbout that the farmers did not meet their obligations. Mr. Duplessis reviewed the other legislation of his government during his three years of rule. His had been a government of heart rather than a government of the golden calf.

For too long Ministers at Quebec had lent their names to dubious schemes which despoiled the people of their savings, and he had passed a law forbidding Ministers to be directors of companies. When Godbout and Mathewson followed in 1939, they had deliberately given false information to the people, and placed false answers in the official report of the House as regards the financial position of the province, he stated.

FALSE STATEMENTS CHARGED

False information had been given as regards the loan made in the United States a month and a half before the 1939 elections, said Mr. Duplessis. Attempts had been made to misrepresent the fact as to that loan and the fact that exchange had gone against Canada because of the war. "There was no war when we borrowed and we had the assurance of Power and others that there would be no war. It was not the National Union Government which declared war on conscription or put Godbout in power," said Mr. Duplessis. Never had there been so many contradictory speeches made at Québec as had been made by Godbout. He was for something one day and against it the next day, especially on the plebiscite and conscription. Mr. Duplessis said the promise against conscription had been given to Quebec and Quebec only. Quebec only could release Ottawa from that promise. There had been constitutional means of having that promise kept, but unfortunately the people had been deceived in 1939 and had put in office McCarthys, moved by strings from Ottawa.

The National Union leader devoted some time to talk on infringements of Quebec rights. Turning to provincial matters he termed the sales tax odious and every woman, who was the treasurer of the home, best knew that fact, he said.

"Ladies, I did not give you the vote, and was against it, but I gave the widows and orphans a chance to live. I will give you a promise now, and we keep our promises, and that is that as soon as we get into power we will abolish the sales tax." Mr. Duplessis said the Godbout Government had raised taxes of 30 millions a year and had no burden of unemployment on their hands having got rid of the unemployment by forcing the unemployed into the Army under penalty of starving.

SAYS QUEBEC LOYAL ENOUGH

The Federal Government had no money for the unemployed, yet had a billion dollars to give England as a present and they are richer than we are. Mr. Duplessis said Quebec wanted no lessons in loyalty from anyone. It had shown its loyalty often enough in the past.

Mr. Duplessis described the Government which he would soon form as one which would not work on routine lines but which respected cardinal principles. It would be a government which would not ration the truth. It would be a government of heart, and justice, and which would take back from Ottawa, no matter who was in power there, the rights which had been filched from the province.

Mr. Duplessis ended in English, remarking that the people who read The Gazette and Montreal Star might think he was a terrible man, he wanted to tell them the National Union Party was not a parochial party.

He had been in power in 1938 when approached by a prominent Montreal lawyer, now dead, and the president of a newsprint company, asking that Anticosti be sold to a German company. He felt certain, he said, that those two gentlemen would not have made the proposal they had if they had realized what was to come. He had told them there was no place for German brutes in this province.

"We are loyal to our oath of allegiance but also loyal to ourselves," said Mr. Duplessis. "I am told I should not talk so much of autonomy. Ulster has its own Parliament and self-government, so has the south of Ireland, and so has Britain, why should we not have self-government in Quebec? There are 48 states with self-government. We are asking for fair play and decency. I know some people don't like me. I don't care. They have a right to their own opinion and I have a right to mine. I have never raised race cries and never will do so. Mr. Godbout last year went into Huntingdon and said Hitler would be glad if my candidate was elected, and then told the people in St. Johns-Napierville I gave too much to the English. I have never used such tactics and will never do so. I want justice for all. We ask fair play and will give fair play," Mr. Duplessis concluded.

Part II

Autonomy: Principles or Politics?

Duplessis' name has always been linked with the demand for autonomy. However, in the nineteenth century Mowat in Ontario and Mercier in Québec, and in the twentieth century contemporaries of Duplessis such as Aberhart in Alberta and Hepburn in Ontario, presented equally strong demands for strengthening provincial governments against centralization.

The question of provincial autonomy arises out of the very nature of the Canadian federation and the interpretation of the original intent of the British North America Act of 1867. Did the Fathers of Confederation establish a strong central government with but weak provincial counterparts, or were the components of Canada made up of equal and sovereign governments?

The history of Canadian Federal-provincial relations has seen periods of strong centralization and periods of active provincialism. During the First World War the role of the Federal government dominated the political life of Canada. After the war, the Federal Liberal Party, traditionally champions of provincial autonomy, under their new leader W. L. M. King allowed greater powers to devolve upon the provinces. The Depression created problems in the realms of social responsibility and distribution of government revenues. Rich provinces wished to retain their revenues to meet their obligations to their citizens; the poorer provinces wanted the Federal government to redistribute wealth so that they, too, could take care of their impoverished citizens. In the middle of the Depression decade a Royal Commission on Federal-provincial relations was established, but its report was not brought in until 1939. By then the requirements of the Second World War led to another period of Federal ascendency, and Ottawa's dominance endured till 1957. This is the context in which Duplessis operated.

The role of the autonomy issue in the Duplessis era has many facets. Roger Lemelin, a French Canadian author, well illustrates the linking of autonomy and nationalism. Québec, not Ottawa, is the homeland. Sentiment, and not politics, is one of the fundamental premises of many French-Canadians' views on autonomy. Duplessis viewed autonomy not merely as a matter of principle, but as a constitutional requirement. His speeches before the Federal-provincial Conferences of 1950 and 1957 make this clear. Some commentators have viewed his demands as a political ploy unleashed to distract the Québec electorate. Wilfrid Eggleston, a well-known Canadian journalist and professor of journalism at Carleton University, calls autonomy a "fetish," while Martin O'Connell, a specialist in Québec history and a journalist, views Duplessis' attitudes as mere electioneering tactics. This view is shared by a member of the National Assembly of Québec, Pierre Laporte. Mr. Laporte was at one time a reporter for *Le Devoir*, and he later became a member of the Liberal government of Jean Lesage.

On the other hand, it may well be asked whether Duplessis, as a spokesman for the government and people of Québec, was honestly and accurately reflecting the will of the majority of his electorate. Economic autonomy is a further facet of the autonomy issue. Father Emile Bouvier, a member of the Economics department of the Université de Sherbrooke, interprets Duplessis' double taxation as being part and parcel of French Canadian nationalism. The English-speaking reaction in Québec here is from the pen of Hugh MacLennan, better known for his novels than for his economic views.

Yet another aspect of the autonomy question is evident in Wilbur Arkinson's article in the *Montreal Gazette*. Arkinson was the paper's Québec staff reporter. The establishment and report of the Tremblay Commission was a matter of politics according to some. It also, however, emphasized an integrated view of the problem—money, culture and nationalism could not be separated.

Evidently, provincial autonomy can mean many things. It can be used for base purposes, in other words, power for Duplessis and the Union Nationale. On the other hand, it must be pointed out that until the federal election of 1968, no political party in Québec has ever presented itself as the champion of a strong federalism and a weak provincialism. Was Duplessis' use of autonomy unique in Québec politics or was it the norm?

Roger Lemelin, "I Keep Away From Ottawa", *Saturday Night,* vol. 66, no. 15, January 16, 1951, p. 11. Reprinted by permission of the Author.

Quebec is my Home Town

"Why," a friend will ask me, "why, Lemelin, do you keep away from Ottawa?"

"What a question!" I reply. "It is as if you suddenly ask me why I have four children."

After six hours and a half of profound thought, I find that a Quebecker like me has many reasons to keep away from Ottawa, as well as a father of four children can give many explanations concerning the number of his descendants. . . .

Quebec City is my home town, and I simply love it. When I was a boy, running away from lower town of Quebec, to explore the fields of the outskirts, skiing in the winter, picking cherries and strawberries (when I was not stealing apples) in the summer, I began at the end of the day to get fed up with pastoral life and to long after the paved streets of my crowded parish. I have not changed. It has always been hard for me to share the nationalism of some of my fellow compatriots for their province, or more scarcely, for Canada as a whole.

I know many educated people in my province, some are my friends, who nearly faint when they pronounce Paris, and who would give all they have (they say so) to die and live there. You probably have some of these distinguished brains who feel the same way about London, England. It has happened to me that I have gone to France as well as to the United States, and each time I longed for Canada, and when I say Canada, I mean Quebec City. And I wonder if this apparently narrow, sentimental love for one's hometown is not the most probing characteristic that indicates true and sincere nationalism. . . .

Have you ever received a letter from Ottawa? Everybody has. There is always a reference, with many figures and that word "department." It makes me shiver. Moreover, the letters OHMS appear on each envelope, and even your closest friends in Ottawa use OHMS paper and envelope. Nobody seems to buy stamps over there. I am one of those guys who enjoy receiving the mail. Each envelope has its mystery. You wonder who is writing to you—maybe it's good news? But when I receive an envelope from Ottawa, I am afraid to open it. You never know. These days, a lot of people get into trouble with the Income Tax Department. When you start getting involved in one of these Ottawa cogwheels, there is no way out. You have to go through the whole machine, and when at last the filing system has settled its problem with you, it abandons you, exhausted, disgusted and poorer.

This summer, I wrote a script for the National Film Board. When time of payment came, I had to advise them. The Production Department referred the matter to the Treasury Department which in turn sent me some sets of forms in quintuplicate to be signed. It cost me 12 cents worth of stamps to return the documents. Some time later I received a cheque from the Treasury and I frowned: it was cut by 15 per cent. I wrote about my surprise to the Chief of the Production Department who referred the matter again to the Department of Treasury, which in turn sent me a T.D.1 form. I filled it, signed it. I received word that my T.D.1 was not accepted by the Department of Income Tax to which it had been referred, and that if I would like to try and fill a new T.D.1, with some alterations, other forms would be sent me, or else I would have to discuss the whole matter with one of the Controllers of Income Tax. I then wrote a sentimental letter to the Controller of the Production Department of the National Film Board. He seemed to understand me, but . . . procedure is procedure.

I did not answer and I sat down for a moment, exhausted, at the maw of this big machine. It is so well greased, but my God, how, in its logical perfection, can it work under the paradoxical ensign of OHMS? I like to feel being a Canadian, but I still do not see how matters stand between Ottawa and His Majesty. Maybe you have to go through 12,589 files before knowing it. And I am too busy down here to check all these files. While we are on the subject, I like clear things. I do not know if you ever considered that, but very complicated things can be made clear. It is often clear that Ottawa does not know how to make clear complicated things. . . .

I do not say that people in Ottawa are boring; I just mean I would get bored to death there. The Ottawa machine is too perfect to have personality. As soon as a brilliant man goes and settles there, taking part in the government of the country, it is as if he became a number in a department. From here, even the Cabinet looks to me like an anonymous corporation. You never know who has pushed forth a decision. I know Mr. Louis St. Laurent and the respect I have for him cannot be deeper. I have seen him walk on the Grande-Allée like the grand gentleman he is, I have talked to him. Sometimes I wonder if he walks the same way in Ottawa. Maybe. Because in Quebec Mr. St. Laurent always knew where he went, and even in Ottawa he probably knows too.

But I am not Mr. St. Laurent, and the promiscuity of the anonymous machine scares me. If a perfect democracy produces such a perfect thing as the Ottawa machine, I prefer to keep at least 300 miles away from this perfect robot. Let me stay where I am, amidst the Quebec cocktail of democracy, autocracy and theocracy. By the way: is there a religion in Ottawa? From here it looks to me that going to heaven or hell is never considered there: only to limbo. . . .

I keep away from Ottawa because, also, I was never offered a good job there.

Proceedings of the Constitutional Conference of Federal and Provincial Governments, January 10-12, 1950, (Ottawa, King's Printer, 1950), pp. 16-17; *Dominion-Provincial Conference, November 25th, 26th, 1957,* (Ottawa, Queen's Printer, 1958), pp. 21-24, 28.

Autonomy: Principles

[M. Duplessis 1950]

In the Province of Quebec we consider that the British North America Act does not create our rights, but only confirms and reasserts the rights of our province. . . .

. . . When Confederation was discussed and decided upon, it was based on the principle of complete provincial autonomy. And this for excellent reasons, the most important of which is that Confederation is not only from its very beginning an agreement between four pioneer provinces but it is a sacred covenant between two great races whose friendly co-operation is essential to the weal and prosperity of all concerned.

This fundamental principle cannot and should not be tampered with. To our mind there cannot be any compromise whatever when it comes to decide the kind of administration suitable to Canada. I firmly and definitely believe that Canada is and should always be a federation of autonomous provinces. Apparently there seems to be agreement on all sides on this point—but in fact this is not so. Some people declare themselves in favour of provincial autonomy but do not seem to agree when we contend that provincial autonomy cannot exist without definite and indispensable fiscal powers and that it is useless to have a declaration of rights if, at the same time, there is no financial and fiscal power to exercise those rights. . . . There are some who, for what seems to us to be excellent reasons, think that the British North America Act is a treaty of union between two great races; others are of the opinion that it is only a law. I firmly believe that Confederation is a treaty of union between two great races. . . . The fact is undeniable that the Canadian constitution is founded essentially and fundamentally upon the agreement of the four pioneer provinces. . . . The Province of Quebec would never have agreed to enter into Confederation had it not been made abundantly clear, at that time, that the guarantees upon which Confederation is based were to remain and last. This opinion is not a personal one, it is not only the opinion of the Province of Quebec; it is the considered opinion of very many Canadian and English statesmen and jurists. . . .

Quebec believes in responsible government and we contend that there cannot be responsible government without indispensable financial powers. Bearing in mind these fundamental principles I am convinced that we can arrive at a fair and appropriate solution of our problems. . . .

[M. Duplessis 1957]

. . . I wish first to thank the Prime Minister of Canada for his courtesy—

his appropriate courtesy—in saying a few words in the French language at the opening of this momentous conference. I am very pleased to thank him and congratulate him. While Mr. King was Prime Minister the Province of Quebec's representatives were never shown the same courtesy. I extend my sincere congratulations to the Prime Minister on this improvement! . . .

. . . as far as Quebec is concerned, we wish to discuss at this Conference a problem of vital importance—the federal-provincial fiscal relations. After all, on this earth money is absolutely necessary to administer and legislate in an appropriate and progressive way.

The first question on the agenda obviously is the problem of federal-provincial fiscal relations; in other words, the equitable and appropriate division of federal and provincial revenue sources. The vitality and progress of a genuinely national harmony, as well as the development of Canada, of the provinces, the municipal, school and parish Corporations, are intimately connected with the solution of this financial problem. . . .

Let us, first of all, remember that in each Province the federal taxpayer is at the same time the provincial, municipal, school and parish ratepayer. What advantage would be gained in having the tax dollar collected for provincial purposes make a wide detour via Ottawa before being returned to us? Would it be any bigger when it reached us after such a journey? Obviously not.

The taxpayer's ability to pay is not limitless and it is necessary that the tax he pays should be suitably levied and divided between the powers, which he supports and on which he depends, so that his spirit of initiative will not be destroyed by unduly onerous assessments. The collection of these taxes is closely linked to the essential function of government and the truth of two well-known axioms is undeniable: "Whoever holds the purse-strings, at all times, exerts the supreme authority", and "The right to tax is the right to govern." . . .

But some people in Ottawa—I am not referring to the members of the present Federal Government—have undoubtedly a centralizing mentality. For instance when federal parliament is mentioned, they use capital "F" and capital "P". But when there is a reference to the provincial legislatures they use very small letters. One may say that this is not important, but just the same it manifests a disrespectful attitude towards provincial legislatures. . . .

It is certain that responsible government can never exist if fiscal powers, which are indispensable to the exercise of the constitutional rights and the performance of the constitutional obligations, are not wedded to legislative and administrative prerogatives. . . .

It is the considered opinion of the Government of the Province of Quebec that the Canadian Constitution, whose foundations should remain untouched, is sufficiently clear, but since doubts on this subject have been expressed by persons of good faith, we suggest it would be useful to dissipate these doubts and this by the three following methods:

1. Clarification and delimitation of the powers of taxation of both the Federal and Provincial authorities, in accordance with the letter and spirit of the Canadian Constitution, that is to say having regard to the past, the present and the future.

2. Simplification of public taxation in such a way as to reduce its cost and facilitate its collection.

3. Moderation in the domain of taxation to be arrived at by the collaboration of all public powers, in such a way as to ease the burden of the taxpayer so far as possible.

Wilfrid Eggleston, "Autonomy Talk Has Limits", *Saturday Night*, vol. 65, no. 15, January 17, 1950, p. 3. Reprinted by permission of the Author.

The Autonomy Fetish

The enthusiasm with which a large number of French-speaking Canadians receive the fighting speeches of Premier Maurice Duplessis, in which he appears as the champion of minority rights and indeed as the Savior of Quebec, is not difficult to understand. From the local and short-term viewpoint, this concern over regional rights may appear wholly admirable, and even a true expression of liberty against a threatening centralization.

As for the "compact theory" of Confederation, it is doubtful whether the masses of the people, whether French-speaking or not, are aware of its implications if once thoroughly accepted as the nature of the Canadian federal union.

Yet it is a safe bet that there are a great many Canadians who are most warmly disposed toward the French-speaking part of Canada. These Canadians are true friends of liberty and thus stoutly opposed to centralized bureaucracy. And yet they are perturbed and saddened at the intransigent attitude taken by the Premier of Quebec and his political party. They are perturbed and saddened because they believe that not only is an extreme or strident provincialism anywhere in Canada destructive of our Canadian unity, but even that it damages the welfare of the very region that it seeks to advance.

NO HAMSTRINGING

A measure of provincial autonomy was intended and in effect guaranteed by the terms of union in 1867. It is fair to say that in the main that measure of provincial autonomy has been preserved and even in some respects notably enhanced. It was never intended that provincial rights should hamstring the operations of the nation as a whole. The Fathers of Confederation were determined about that. It is when the cry of provincial autonomy begins to menace the welfare of the whole nation that it becomes alarming to the Canadian whose first loyalty is to his country.

As Premier McNair put it at the 1945 Conference:

"One should not recognize provincial autonomy, so-called, as an end in itself. It may easily become a fetish, a catch-cry, or a cloak for regional, or sectional advantage and privilege. The primary end of all government in Canada is the welfare of the people."

It would be a great service to Canada if someone would persuade a few of the *Union Nationale* leaders to spend a few months in other parts of Canada, so as to attain a national rather than provincial outlook. One of the unfortunate consequences of a too shrill provincialist agitation in Quebec is the emotion aroused in other parts of the country. This sometimes finds angry or indiscreet expression. This in turn is reproduced in the autonomist press of Quebec, and there it serves to convince additional people that Quebec has enemies in other parts of Canada against which it must be guarded.

An illustration of the reaction aroused in other parts of Canada by extreme autonomist doctrines is provided by an editorial in the Edmonton *Journal* in 1948, just after Premier Duplessis and his party had been returned to office with an overwhelming majority.

GO ALONE?

This said, in part: "The effect of Quebec's vote will be felt outside of Quebec more than within it . . . in federal affairs, the Duplessis sweep will strengthen the hands of the Ontario-Quebec 'axis,' which means a still bitterer opposition to federal-provincial tax agreements, to any further attempt by the Dominion Government to make the national economy truly national.

"Duplessis can offer his tremendous support at the polls as evidence enough that the French-Canadian province intends to 'go alone' and will fight to the limit any suggestion that the nation is superior to any of its parts . . . We may soon see the wealthy central-provinces arrayed more stoutly against the western and maritime provinces. If this does develop, national unity and a more healthy economic and political relationship between federal and provincial administrations will be given, not a mortal, but a severe blow."

Federalism is in essence a compromise: the parties that unite know that to form a new nation they must give up some of their autonomy, in return for the gains promised by amalgamation with other parties. Quebec has gained enormously since 1867 by its intimate integration within the new northern nation thus formed, of which it continues to form a vital part. To talk as though all the attributes and advantages of a completely independent state can again be enjoyed while sharing all the other advantages of membership in a great new nation is illogical: an attempt to eat one's cake and have it too.

Emile Bouvier, s.j., "Pourquoi l'impôt provincial sur le revenu?", *Relations,* no. 150, mars 1954, pp. 63-65. (tr.) Reprinted by permission of *Relations.*

No Autonomy without Taxation

When the Prime Minister announced to journalists on 5 February [1954] that the province would institute a provincial personal income tax, a murmur of general disapproval spread through the business offices of the metropolis. People everywhere asked: why a new tax? Why not accept the Federal government's offer? Why a double taxation? . . .

Quebec's financial position is far better than that of any other Canadian province; its net *per capita* debt is the lowest (with the exception of Newfoundland); its total debt has fallen from $308 millions (1945) to $273 millions (1953), in a period of rising prices. The proof of Quebec's financial stability lies in the fact that it can borrow on the New York market at an interest rate lower than that exacted for the financing of the loans of any other province.

Thus, why institute new taxes? In point of fact, Quebec does not want to impose new taxes, it wants to transfer old ones. It is simply taking back those powers of taxation that article 92 of the B.N.A. Act conferred upon it, and that the Federal government borrowed from it in 1941. In April 1941, when requesting these powers, the Hon. J. L. Ilsley stated definitely: "It is proposed, therefore, as a temporary expedient, for the duration of the war only . . . I should like to emphasize that this is not an attempt to get the provinces out of these fields permanently . . ." The provinces agreed to this temporary concession as part of the war effort; they signed it freely, without any coercion, and without having their hand forced.

Unfortunately, the Federal government, having maintained the war-time fiscal arrangements for too long, has taken its time in carrying out its promises and in respecting its work, to such an extent that gradually, through the use of subsidies, it has encroached upon the areas of education, hospitalization and social security, areas reserved to the provinces. . . . The provinces were in the process of ceding their autonomy and their rights for a 'mess of [pottage]'. Since 1946, Quebec has always been unwilling to accept this centralization game. . . . Short-sighted people have denigrated Quebec and its government because it refused federal subsidies to universities . . . Now, by a positive act, the government is taking back its rights in the field of taxation. . . .

What are the advantages and the merits of this law?

1. It spares the worker, unlike the Federal law. If his income is below $4,000 the head of a family with two children does not pay any provincial tax. Of the 600,000 taxpayers in Quebec, about 9% have a taxable income exceeding $5,000, and about 3% an income exceeding $10,000. By taxing this privileged class, the law satisfies the demands of distributive justice.

2. In no way does it inflict a loss on the Federal government. In 1953, Ottawa raised . . . $698,658,372 in taxes in Quebec, 41% in the form of income taxes . . . and 55%, corporation taxes . . . Quebec wants to reserve the right to deduct $22-25 million from the $296 million raised by the federal income tax. This does not seem excessive. . . .

This new law orients in a decisive fashion federal-provincial relations towards decentralization and provincial autonomy . . . thereby correcting a disorder which threatens the security of Confederation.

Hugh MacLennan, "A New Tax for Quebec", *Saturday Night,* vol. 69, no. 23, March 13, 1954, p. 9. Reprinted by permission of the Author.

Curses on the New Tax

Montreal, already the most expensive city in Canada, is going to become still more so, for most of the weight of the new provincial income tax is going to fall on it. Some of the language evoked here by this new tax is unprintable in a family magazine, but when visitors ask us why we put up with it we smile ruefully and tell them that Premier Duplessis has proved once more that he knows precisely what he is doing.

That the Premier was within his constitutional rights in imposing a provincial income tax is unquestionable. He was equally within his rights when he refused to accept federal aid for Quebec's hard-pressed universities. But it took more than mere panache for a public servant to run counter to informed and responsible public opinion and to feel secure while he did so.

However limited may be the Premier's understanding of the rest of Canada, his understanding of his own province is profound, and the park benches of politics are crowded with the slumping forms of the men who have underrated it. A controversial figure always, he has made himself the focus and the expression of emotions and attitudes deep within his people. Maurice Duplessis is more than a mere provincial premier and knows it. In the placid meadow of Canadian politics he stands in a class by himself—passionate, brilliant, impulsive, defiant, ruthless and feared.

Even the jokes told about the Premier highlight the extremely personal character of his regime. As this new income tax has been justified as a necessity for Quebec's higher education, last year's story about the inspector of schools has been revived.

"Qui vous a donné cette belle école?" demanded an inspector of the pupils on the opening day of a new school.

"C'est Maurice, qui donne!" was the chanted answer.

The inspector pointed to the piles of shiny new text books. *"Qui vous a donné ces beaux livres?"*

"C'est Maurice, qui donne!"

The inspector strode to the window and pointed outside. *"Qui vous a donné les arbres—le soleil—la belle rivière labas?"*

After a brief silence one small hand went up.

"Oui, mon petit?" said the inspector with an encouraging smile.

"Peut-être—le bon Dieu?"

Before the inspector could correct him, the boys on either side jumped on him, carried him bodily to the door and threw him out. *"Maudit p'tit Rouge!"* they said as they went back to their seats.

How it has come about that Premier Duplessis has reached the position where such jokes are inevitable is the most important single story in Canadian politics since the war. It is a perfect illustration of the old principle that ideas always lag behind events, while emotions lag behind ideas.

Ever since Confederation, the most successful figures in Quebec politics have been those who collaborated with Ottawa. But with the exception of Sir Wilfrid Laurier, none of them received at home the measure of love poured out on men like Henri Bourassa, who dedicated their lives to the defence of the *Canadien* legend, to the comfort of the *Canadien's* chronic feeling of insecurity, to resistance against the pressure of the English-speaking majority which had caused that insecurity.

The Quebec nationalist was an idealist, nor was he as unreasonable as he often sounded. In effect he said to the rest of us: "Acknowledge yourselves as Canadians, and not as British colonials, and our opposition will cease."

When the rest of Canada took that advice, when English-speaking Canadians from Halifax to Victoria discovered a new, independent delight in Canada as a whole, above all when they began to voice an especial pride and affection for Quebec itself, the nationalist found himself without a policy that made sense to anybody. He had won a victory, but it was a victory which had brought him a humiliating reward. He was in the position of a man who has trained himself to press with all his might against a wall and suddenly discovers the wall is no longer there.

But Quebec's old habit of resistance, the conditioned reflex of responses developed over the years, inevitably lingered long after the other provinces had mended their ways. And Maurice Duplessis, infinitely abler and more practical than Bourassa ever was, himself trained like an athlete to fight for his people against all comers, needed a better target than shadows from the past against which the traditional resistance of Quebec could be directed.

He discovered it in something all too tangible—in sheer material bigness.

What is the biggest bureaucracy, the biggest single business in Canada? The Federal Government, of course. And should Quebec, who in her own eyes has borne so long the heat and burden of the day, acknowledge herself beholden to the Johnnies-come-lately who have just now discovered a truth which has been obvious to the *Québecois* for more than a century?

It is one thing to feel this way; it is quite another to translate such a feeling into practical politics. It is the measure of Maurice Duplessis' political genius that this is precisely what he has done, and on a variety of levels.

To the farmer he appears as a champion of the old rural ways against the cities which entice his sons off the land into the factory; that is why the Premier can fight Catholic labor syndicates without losing the support of the village *curés*. To not a few businessmen, English as well as French, his strong hand has seemed a guarantee against unions, especially American-dominated ones, no less than against undue American or federal exploitation of Quebec's resources. To a people with whom resistance to majorities is a habit of mind, the very violence with which the Premier strikes back at his critics has a certain appeal, for generally his critics are identified with a group alien to the bulk of those who vote for *Union Nationale*.

Now, as a coping stone to his edifice of provincial autonomy, the Premier has insisted on his constitutional right to collect income taxes, regardless of how much extra money it will cost the taxpayer, of how much inconvenience it will bring upon the employer, of how many extra employees will have to be added to the provincial payroll—and few farmers will have to pay the tax anyway! But the money, the Premier insists, is needed. As he passionately declared all along, the universities of Quebec *will* get the assistance they require. But from Quebec, not from Ottawa. *C'est Maurice, qui donne!*

Meanwhile in Montreal one wonders how long this curious, emotional state of affairs is going to last, and people ask each other if life in Montreal is going to be hobbled by double taxation permanently.

This fear, real enough at the moment, is probably unfounded, and for an elementary reason. Though ideas lag behind events, and emotions behind ideas, history would never move at all if the last cars in the train did not eventually reach the points the locomotive has already passed.

That is why it is more important now than it ever was for the rest of Canada to understand the true position of affairs in the key province. In the last cars of the train the conductor punching the tickets is the provincial premier, but up in the cab of the new, streamlined Diesel engine sits another citizen of Quebec, the Prime Minister of Canada itself.

Martin P. O'Connell, "Duplessis in Deflation", *Canadian Forum,* vol. XXXIV, no. 406, November 1954, pp. 171-172. Reprinted by permission of the Author.

Duplessis is a Grave Inconvenience to Ottawa

Nothing has so quickened political currents in Canada in the past month as M. St. Laurent's sallies against the Premier of Quebec. The most urgent reasons, however, behind those attacks have not yet been fully explored.

The balance of political factors scarcely supports the vigor and sweeping range of the Prime Minister's remarks, important as those factors have been. His timing, no doubt, has been admirable. He joined battle when his personal prestige and that of the federal government were never higher; he caught M. Duplessis at a time when the strains on the latter's power structure had become serious. . . .

He has forced M. Duplessis to the conference table when two successive budget deficits have highlighted the latter's need for additional revenue to maintain the province's expansion in all spheres, and before the Union Nationale leader could avail himself of the findings of his Royal Commission on constitutional problems (the Tremblay Commission).

M. Duplessis has been a grave inconvenience to Ottawa, anxious as it is to round the corners of the new federalism, but this does not explain the kind of attack delivered by M. St. Laurent. Was then the Prime Minister trying only to make smooth the way of his successor? If so, he had small chance of success, particularly if he engaged in a protracted battle with M. Duplessis on issues that can easily be formulated in terms of provincial autonomy. He would leave Quebec-Ottawa relations embittered, and he would almost certainly lose electoral support in Quebec for both the federal and provincial Liberal parties. Already he has surprised and embarrassed the provincial Liberals, who have no policy of their own on the tax question, and who do not in any case want to confront M. Duplessis once again on federal issues on which they have been soundly beaten in three successive general elections. . . .

More urgent considerations than these propelled M. St. Laurent forward, and they may be better understood by the economists in the Finance Department than by the rest of us. For it is in the economic order that conditions essential to the central government's performance of its functions in the new federalism have most altered, and it is there that further explanations of the Prime Minister's conduct may be sought. . . .

Federal government policies of economic stabilization at high levels of employment and income (a leading principle of the new federalism) require from Quebec in a period of deflation a different and greater order of co-operation than has been essential over the past decade when quite other economic conditions prevailed, and when policies to combat inflation were developed. In order that the central government may use effectively the fiscal, monetary, and other economic mesaures designed by Keynesian economists to enable it to act as a balance in the economy, smoothing out severe fluctuations, it must keep open, if not expand, as many channels of expenditure as it can command under the constitution, or through agreements with the provinces. Particularly important is the power to determine the level of taxation in the principal fields, which are open to joint occupancy by the federal and provincial governments. Such control is necessary partly for the sake of revenues for national purposes, and to enable the federal government to balance surpluses in one period against deficits in another, and partly for the sake of manipulation so as to stimulate economic activity or reduce inflationary pressures. In all instances but that of Quebec, this power has been secured to the federal government for a five-year period by a series of agreements by which the provinces rent to it their right to share the principal tax fields, including income tax, in return for guaranteed annual payments. . . .

Moreover, had these provinces levied income taxes, the effects would have been anti-inflationary, and thus in accord with the direction of national policies. But if the period of deflation and of deficit financing approaches, then provinces levying income taxes at rates that escape control by the federal government may neutralize, or prevent the adoption of, anti-deflationary policies by the federal government. That this would have important adverse political effects in the country as a whole seems evident. In such circumstances it becomes urgent for Ottawa to gain some control over M. Duplessis' income tax, and this can be done if Ottawa is willing to pass beyond the rental formulas and incorporate into the framework of agreements a provincial income tax at an agreed-upon rate of deduction from the levels set by the federal authorities. The prospects of this occurring now seem bright.

At the present time it is not the immediate fiscal effects of M. Duplessis' income tax that causes most concern; it is the implications for the future of the doctrine of provincial priority in direct tax fields, and the demand for total deductibility which he advanced with his tax. The doctrine of priority implies the right to exclude completely the federal government from direct taxes, which makes nonsense of its constitutional right to raise money by "any mode" of taxation. The demand for total deductibility of the provincial from the federal income tax could mean in an extreme case a provincial claim to the whole of the income tax collected by the federal government within the province. Both claims undermine the existing structure of tax agreements and the capacity of the federal government to discharge its functions. Naturally enough, they will not be conceded by M. St. Laurent. Both, however, can readily be abandoned by M. Duplessis now that they have served their purpose of putting Ottawa in a more tractable frame of mind in which to consider the deductibility principle as an alternative to the rental formula. The rental formula Duplessis will not accept since, reasonably enough, he sees a weakening of provincial autonomy in arrangements by which provinces give over the chief financial means of their independence. But there is sufficient reason to expect that he will come to terms in a tax agreement based on a level of deduction which will yield sums to Quebec roughly equal to what she would receive under a rental scheme. The exact level of exemption and deduction, the variation of the level from year to year, and the time such an agreement should run are matters of negotiation, but they should be related to the results achieved under the rental agreements. From the standpoint of Ottawa the costs would be no different, but more important, it would have gained what it deems essential—control over the level of income taxation in Quebec. It would be for it to set the total income tax burden, which does not now obtain, and for M. Duplessis to receive a stipulated share. If such a settlement emerges from the recent struggle, the federal government will have improved its ability to employ fiscal policy in its own and the national interest, and M. Duplessis, on his part, will have found a formula to reconcile provincial autonomy with national needs. While obtaining fiscal justice Quebec would be contributing in its own way to the transfer of wealth from some provinces to others to an extent comparable to that possible under the rental agreements.

If M. Duplessis presents a different and more difficult problem in deflation, then the Prime Minister's task has been to sharpen the issues, to throw a protective screen around the federal government's necessities, and to induce M. Duplessis to accept a lower price for cooperation than was hitherto demanded. This he seems to have accomplished.

Pierre Laporte, "Le Rapport Tremblay . . .", *L'Action Nationale*, vol. XLVII, no. 2, October 1957, pp. 113-118. (tr.) Reprinted by permission of *L'Action Nationale.*

Autonomy Equals Politics

The Tremblay Report consists of five volumes. It is a document of 2,000 pages. It constitutes the most formidable study of constitutional problems ever prepared in the province of Quebec. . . .

. . . the Prime Minister of the province had not been won over beforehand to the idea of an inquiry on provincial autonomy. This will not astound anyone who is familiar with Mr. Duplessis' personality. He has an almost superstitious love for the *déjà vu,* the *status quo.* He likes to tell the following story: A liberal deputy went to see Prime Minister Taschereau to propose a reform. The latter answered: "Did your constituents ask you for this?" "No," replied the deputy. "Then why put it into their heads," concluded the Prime Minister.

Such was Mr. Duplessis' mentality. Provincial autonomy served his political ends well. Why then push his luck by concerning himself too closely with this subject?

It was ultimately public opinion that forced his hand to some extent.

It is well known that Mr. Duplessis loves nice little inquiries that come to naught. He sets up commissions in order to find a place for friends and so arranges matters that nothing more is ever heard of them. Those few inquiries that do come to something generally praise the government and are made public just in time for an election campaign. He no doubt hoped that the Tremblay Commission would assume the same *tempo* as other commissions and would disappear into oblivion forever. . . .

We know what happened: the commissioners travelled all around the province, seriously studied the problem and submitted an impressive report.

Normally the submission of the report would have been the object of a solemn ceremony. The document would have been put before the Legislative Assembly and studied by a committee. But no. Four months passed before the Prime Minister made public only a few of the secrets of the Tremblay Report. It was impossible, even for the press, to obtain copies through the ordinary channels. The pretext was that an English version was awaited before the report was distributed. It had been translated and printed, but the French copies remained on ice in Quebec. The Chamber of Commerce of the Province of Quebec managed to obtain 200 copies. It is said that certain other public bodies also received a few copies. But the bulk of the edition has not been offered to the public. This document is almost on the index of our political literature!

Wilbur Arkison, "New Vision Says Commission", *Montreal Gazette,* Saturday, April 7, 1956.

New Vision

The Quebec Royal Commission of Inquiry on Constitution Problems today recommended that Quebec should invite the Federal Government and other provinces to undertake jointly a re-adaptation of the public administration according to the spirit of federalism.

This re-shaping, the Commission urged, would be carried out "within the framework of the Constitution, and would aim at re-interpreting its master-ideas in the four major provisions which a fiscal policy for our times, conforming both to federalism and to the state's general needs, ought to provide."

The six-man commission, headed by Judge Thomas Tremblay of the Quebec Court of Sessions, outlined the following general recommendations:

1. The primary purpose of Canadian federalism is to allow the two great cultural communities which make up our population (a) to live and develop themselves according to their respective particularisms; and (b) to co-operate in the building and progress of a common Fatherland;

2. With regard to French-Canadian culture, the Province of Quebec assumes alone the responsibilities which the other provinces jointly assume with regard to Anglo-Canadian culture;

3. The Canadian reality, both economic and sociological, has undergone a profound transformation since 1867, but its cultural elements have not changed, so that the basic problem still remains the same.

Furthermore:

4. (a) Transformation and integration of the economic and social complex have made economic stability one of the major political goals; (b) ideas regarding the state's economic and social role have also evolved, with intervention by the state in the economy's functioning being today admissible, both in theory and in practice, while a new school of economists claim it can give it a scientific basis and standards. . . ;

5. Industrial concentration has created fiscal inequalities as between the provinces, and these should be remedied, insofar as possible;

6. Control of the economy and equalization of fiscal conditions as between the provinces are the main reason today invoked by the Federal Government as justifying its social as well as its fiscal policy. It considers both of these, over and beyond their special purposes, as being indispensable instruments of economic control.

The Federal Government, moreover, relies on an interpretation of the constitution according to which it is vested with the main economic powers, and possesses "unlimited" power to tax and "absolute" power to spend. Thus, it concludes that it alone can exercise all initiatives needed to control the economy, to maintain employment, and to equalize the fiscal resources between the provinces. As a consequence it seems to think that pursuit of economic and social goals has, in some way, priority over cultural objectives, and also that the Federal Government itself has similar priority over the provinces.

Such is the basic conflict of which the fiscal problem is the most visible manifestation. . . . In short, it arises from a unitary and non-federative interpretation of the Constitution and of the very notion of a state, and it arises also from a technically administrative but non-political concept of the state's role in economic and social affairs. . . .

"For our power," the commission added, "we hold there is no opposition between the state's economic and social goals and its cultural objectives and we believe both of them can be effectively realized in a federative system, provided there is an awareness of the political nature of the problem and of the steps that must be taken in order to ensure a harmonious solution in a country as differentiated as Canada."

The report states that politics, in the best sense of the word, has for its objective not merely welfare but good living which it states is the "hierarchic totality of conditions needed for full assertion of human individuality." . . .

"In the federative state of the cultural type," the report adds, "they should be distributed between the orders of government according to the function with which they are vested.

"Thus, since taxes on income have a direct incidence on persons and institutions, they should belong to the government on which cultural and social responsibility is incumbent.

"Since taxes on business operations and on the circulation of goods have a direct economic incidence, and, if employed on the regional and local level, would tend to raise barriers within the same country, they should logically belong to that government which is vested with the larger economic responsibility and whose jurisdiction extends over the whole country.

"If equality of services between the several parts of a federative state is desirable it cannot, however, be considered an absolute.

"Consequently, it cannot be established as a permanent system for the redistribution of funds, nor, more especially, can it be sought to the detriment of higher interests of one or more groups," the report asserted.

Martin P. O'Connell, "M. Duplessis' Royal Commission", *Canadian Forum,* vol. XXXVI, no. 425, June 1956, pp. 50-52. Reprinted by permission of the Author.

The Tremblay Commission: A Tactical Blunder

At first glance the recommendations of the Tremblay Commission on constitutional problems appear a tactical blunder on the part of Quebec nationalists. It is doubtful that M. Duplessis will give them prominence in the forthcoming June elections, though he may well emphasize the new sociological dimensions the Commission gives the autonomist faith, and he may promise the permanent research organizations it suggested: a Natural Resources Council, a Commission in Aid of Higher Education, and a Provincial Council of Arts and Letters. The Report unexpectedly threw nationalism on the defensive. It wrote into an official document a clear statement of principles and aims and, in the name of the "spirit of federalism", it proposed an extravagant reshaping of fiscal structures which would involve such wrenching of the federal system that few responsible leaders are likely to support it. There will also be serious doubts that the fiscal proposals in the Report would in fact aid in achieving legitimate goals of autonomy, social welfare, cultural development, and economic stability, although the Commissioners state that the "whole population of Quebec" wanted no mere redistribution of funds to carry on government but a basic reappraisal of lasting requirements, and that it gave a "practically unanimous" response to the inquiry. . . .

The Commission's fiscal policy displays a refreshing interest in first principles, philosophical and sociological, though the results may not recommend themselves to politicians and federal economists. Thus, starting from the personalist concept, in which Man is accorded primacy (as opposed to the totalitarian concepts of socialism and fascism in which the state comes first) there is derived the proposal that governments in Canada should establish a maximum tax burden at some specified percentage of the national income. This would enable citizens and institutions to live and exercise proper initiatives. Once a maximum level of taxes is agreed upon, the federal and provincial governments should then share direct taxation according to a rule dictated by the qualitative effects of taxation on collective life, and according to the functions vested in them by the "sociological reality" which they represent. From these latter principles flows a separatist plan which gives personal and corporate income taxes and estate taxes to the exclusive use of the provinces, exclusive employment of sales taxes, amusement taxes, gasoline and tobacco taxes, and other taxes on goods and the circulation of goods. In this way federal "encroachments" in the direct tax field would cease, the "drain" of public funds "regain" what is theirs by right. Thus, too, would the Spirit of the Constitution triumph notwithstanding the unequivocal constitutional right of the federal government to any mode of taxation whatever.

This reversal of current fiscal arrangements would be followed by a complete shift of social security to the provinces. Under the Tremblay plan, the provinces would finance old age pensions, family allowances, veterans' pensions, unemployment insurance, etc. The Commissioners considered it especially important that Quebec exercise such social welfare functions because the provincial government constitutes the national focus of French Canada, and because in modern life a national culture is no longer perpetuated automatically but is the product of a "conscious and voluntary adhesion to a certain general concept of life and of the value proceeding therefrom." It falls therefore to provincial governments, or at least to the Quebec government, to erect and finance a structure of welfare compatible with the diverse ways of life which constitute Canada. . . .

To the objection that the federal government requires control of tax levels and access to the principal tax fields for policies of economic stability and high employment, the Commission protests that its plan leaves nothing to be desired. It gives the federal government exclusive control of taxes affecting business (though not the corporation tax!) and thus power to influence economic movements. To the provinces, which respond to the collectivity's "stable needs," are assigned the most stable taxes. The provinces would take a leading part in anti-cyclical policy by instituting public works programs to correct unemployment in their respective economies. They would require not only the swollen funds foreseen by the Commission, but access to borrowing at the Bank of Canada, on whose Board of Directors they would place representatives.

Such is the ideal solution. Recogniz ing certain frictions, the Commission also advanced an "Intermediate Solution", and a "Temporary Solution". Under the former, the federal government would continue to participate to a limited degree in social security and to share the corporation income tax since this tax is seen to have the least direct influence on individuals and ways of life. (But reluctantly . . . because in the event of a socializing government attaining power at Ottawa this tax would be used to implant its system.) Under the Temporary Plan, patterned after the 1947 proposals of the *Chambre de Commerce de Montréal,* the federal government would retain responsibility for the great measures of social security now in effect, and both orders of government would share income taxes at levels determined by themselves provided that the provincial tax be deducted from the federal levy, and that a maximum limit of taxes be established. This Temporary Plan, which is not far removed from the thinking of the federal authorities, is conceded by the Commissioners to offer very great advantages in that it "submits the fiscal system to the sole will of the federal government, thereby putting the two orders of government back on an equal footing". Thus, if the Report holds any clue to M. Duplessis' future course of action, it is likely to be found in the Temporary Plan which involves the minimum disturbance of the status quo, and satisfies autonomist sentiment.

The strength of the Tremblay Report lies in its research studies, while its weakness lies in the recommendations. The dismantling of the present structure of social welfare and of the instruments of economic and fiscal control will appeal to few. The effects of the fiscal proposals of the Commission would be incalculable. They would be felt in defence and foreign policy, in the growth of the Canadian economy, and they would tend to increase inflationary pressures in good times and deflationary pressures in recessions. Neither the fiscal plan nor the social welfare proposals of the Commission are the *sine qua non* of provincial autonomy, and in the event of economic disaster, might well induce greater centralization than now exists. Little support will be found among the less favoured provinces for a plan which makes them dependent on the aid of other provinces over which they have no political power. Nor would the plan be reassuring to business which would find one set of governments taxing its income while another taxed its sales, and both tried to co-ordinate policies of stabilization and expansion.

All this does not dispute the essential point, which the Commission could have made more directly, that substantial fiscal readjustments must be made in the near future to enable provinces and municipalities to meet the needs of their expanding economies and social services. But it hardly requires an overturning of the fiscal system and an experiment in disjointed federalism. The Commission has over-stressed the autonomy question and underestimated national requirements. Contradictions in the Commission's argument indicate the weakness of its position, as when the twin statements are made that Quebec is unanimous for autonomy through a reshaped fiscal system, and that the federal government (based largely on unwavering Quebec support) has followed a persistent policy of centralization for thirty years.

Perhaps the most significant feature of the Report is the evidence of a shift from cultural defence to cultural development. This properly leads to concern with the financial and constitutional means thereto, and is wholly welcome. Most Canadians accept the thesis of cultural dualism though they need education in ways of fostering it. The Commission's studies are a step in that direction, but its plan will meet the same fate as other neatly rounded general solutions to continuing problems in Canada.

Part III

The Economic Man: Exploiter or Exploited?

Duplessis' supporters and critics agree that the Premier, his party and his policies had a significant effect on the economy of Québec. His champions claim that he was instrumental in creating an environment that attracted industry to the province and thus increased employment and government revenues. The implication is that without Duplessis there would have been less or little economic growth. His critics suggest, and at times overtly declare, that economic development could have been greater had they been in power, or that it could have taken place on better terms. Further, Duplessis' purposes were personal and political rather than social.

These claims and counter claims isolate the issue of economic development in Québec during the Duplessis regime. They neglect the economic growth of the province prior to the Duplessis era and the conditions peculiar to the period 1936 to 1959. Both also underplay the dominant contemporary ideologies of Québec, Canada and North American society. As well, too little consideration is given to the narrowness of the available options. The man is emphasized, not the context.

Economic development and growth in Québec, in particular since 1896, closely followed the Canadian pattern. The rate of economic and industrial development in Central Canada, that is Québec and Ontario, is very similar. The two provinces are one unit of an economy whose dominant characteristic is economic regionalism. Both of the central provinces, regardless of the party in power in each, were the main beneficiaries of the economic system that has been called the 'new industrialism'.

One of the primary characteristics of the 'new industrialism' is the growth of *capital-intensive industries*. The 'old industrialism' had as one of its chief characteristics *labour-intensive industries*. Industrial investment in Québec and Ontario in the 20th century, in sectors such as hydro-electric development, mining, pulp and paper industries and manufacturing plants, has required large capital outlays. The usual economic institution was the corporation. Money was raised by the sale of common stock and bonds. Both provinces granted economic privileges such as tax exemptions or low royalty payments in order to attract investment to their provinces.

The Liberal regimes of Lomer Gouin and Louis-Alexandre Taschereau, in power prior to the Duplessis era, adhered to this economic norm. Duplessis and his cohorts of *l'Action libérale nationale* decried *the trusts'* all too personal relations with the Liberal Party, and they used this cry as a political weapon in the 1935 and 1936 elections. As a result, the Union Nationale was viewed by some as a means to economic and social reform. The first two selections of this section, drawn from *Saturday Night* and the writings of Lorenzo Dutil, illustrate this phenomenon. The text from the "Electoral Catechism" in Part I has already presented the close personal relations of the Taschereau family with the capitalist establishment. Another facet is evident in the reading titled "The Chickens Come Home to Roast": economic provincialism. It is noteworthy that the policies of the Liberal government of Ontario differed not one whit from those of the Union Nationale in Québec. They shared common economic problems and solutions.

The dominant economic ideology prevalent in Québec during the Duplessis era, as well as in North America generally, is exposed by the Premier in the reading drawn from *"Industrial Canada"*. Notwithstanding the hue and cry against trusts, or the vocal reform movements and the 'new deals', the political and economic doctrines of the times had as ends the modification of the more exploitative tendencies of the free enterprise and capitalist system, not its abolition. Another purpose was the realization of greater economic benefits for the province: a form of French-Canadian economic nationalism. It is for this end that Duplessis decries the 'pure exploitation' in the selection from the *Montreal Gazette*. In these two selections Duplessis clearly exposes two views: one is very favourable to the free enterprise system; the other just as clearly threatens government intervention to limit it.

Duplessis' threat was more than empty words. The selection on Bill 28 reveals an interesting feature of Anglo-Saxon press reactions to Québec economic legislation. Matters of an economic order, by some kind of subtle transubstantiation, become questions of civil liberties. Other noteworthy features are the passivity of the press in Québec, the society's apparent indifference to curtailment of 'civil liberties', and the economic benefits accruing to Québec from the legislation. Perhaps the oddest feature of the controversy is that implicit in the text selected from the *Canadian Forum*. A socialist journal appears as the defender of the entrenched newsprint monopolists. This legislation reveals the complexity of interests and purposes so characteristic of Duplessis, his party and his society. Was it Duplessis who was exploiting his society, or the society exploiting the commercial establishment; or the commercial elite exploiting Duplessis and Québec society? Why did the masses accept and why did the business community behave so passively? And why did the Anglo-Saxon press outside Québec react so violently?

The *Monetary Times* credits Québec's development to the Premier. This fulsome praise is no doubt to be expected from a journal representative of the economic establishment. Miriam Chapin, a specialist on Québec affairs whose writings are 'popular', accuses Duplessis and his party of selling out the province. This view was shared by some in Québec and many outside of Québec. The quarrel was over the development of the iron deposits in northern Québec. The existence of the deposits was known in the late 19th century, but transportation difficulties and the availability of the ores of the Messassabi range retarded their exploitation. In the early 1950's an American-Canadian consortium was granted the right to develop the deposits. Supplies were flown in; the federal government contributed a deep water port and all of its facilities as its share. A desolate area of the province became the hub of an industrial centre: over 200 million dollars were invested. If this is exploitation, what was its nature? Were other means available to the same ends? And last, was this but cynical exploitation of the resources by Duplessis for personal ends only?

The Québec Natural Gas scandal appears to be a less controversial issue. There is no question that some members of Duplessis' cabinet, the Legislative Assembly and the Legislative Council bought stock on options. It is no less clear that members of the Liberal party also participated, as did many other citizens of the province of Québec, and other provinces. Just how deeply people other than members of the Union Nationale were involved was not revealed until after Duplessis' death, when the Salvas Commission, which investigated the matter, reported its findings. No legal proceedings were instituted on the basis of conflicts of interests over the Québec Natural Gas deal. It is noteworthy that Duplessis himself was never, then or later, personally involved in the scandal. On the other hand *Le Devoir* was never sued for defamation or libel notwithstanding some threats to do so. The scandal simply died a silent, natural death.

Personal, political and economic morality were no doubt moot matters in the Gas scandal. One must, however, note the standards of the times and place the issue in its context. Both Alberta and Ontario also had scandals involving pipelines. In what ways did Québec differ from other provinces in such matters? Another aspect of the problem is the commercial system and business ethics. Is there a difference between ethical behaviour and legal behaviour?

The last reading is drawn from a pamphlet written by Paul Bouchard and used by the Union Nationale in its political campaigns. He proves, statistically at least, that there was absolute economic growth in Québec during the Duplessis era. Industrial progress continued all through the Duplessis regimes. The province had one of the lowest per capita debts in Canada. This strong credit position was used by the Liberal successors of Duplessis in the early 1960's to acquire further capital. However, in the last few years, Québec has had to pay higher and higher interest on its bonds. Economic growth and investment in Québec have fallen significantly below the level prevalent in Ontario. One may well ask if Québec's achievements were due to Duplessis and his party?

Duplessis' policies and the options available to him were defined both by himself and his society. It is in this context that we must attempt to determine who exploited whom and for what purposes.

"The Front Page", *Saturday Night,* vol. 52, no. 30, May 29, 1937, p. 1. Reprinted by permission of *Saturday Night.*

The Chickens Come Home to Roast

The action of the Province of Quebec in prohibiting the granting of any rights in connection with Quebec Crown lands to any company not incorporated in that Province appears to us to be extremely unwise, extremely detrimental to the growth of national unity in Canada, and quite certain to provoke reprisals of a kind which will harm business interests in the Province itself and promote a general feeling of antagonism between Provinces throughout the Dominion. Further than this, the action of the Province of Quebec in refusing the renewal of old-standing licenses held by extra-provincial companies is a gross breach of what has always been regarded as constituting, at any rate during good behavior, a permanent and unassailable property right, a right moreover upon the strength of which many millions of dollars have been invested in permanent plants in the Province of Quebec and many thousands of jobs have thus been made available to Quebec citizens. This is our view, very strongly held, and we are free to express it and shall continue to express it. It is due to no feeling against the Province of Quebec itself, for we have expressed it against other Provinces which have violated the principle of the free movement and equal treatment of capital as between the Provinces, and we shall continue to do so.

But there are certain persons and institutions which have no right to protest against this action by the Province of Quebec. The Province of Ontario has no right to protest against it. The Premier of Ontario has no right to protest against it, and since he is a man of considerable intelligence we predict that he will not protest against it. Individuals and newspapers which have supported the action of the Ontario Government in regard to the Quebec power contracts have no right to protest. The interests which own such newspapers, whatever they may be, have no right to protest.

The Province of Ontario, under the Hepburn Government, started this business of the abolition of property rights belonging to persons or corporations in other Provinces. The action of the Province of Quebec in refusing the renewal of licenses to extra-provincial companies is merely the exercise of a right which was implicitly reserved to it in the grant of the original licenses, although it has always been assumed as a matter of good faith that it would not exercise that right during the good behavior of the licensee. The action of the Province of Ontario in tearing up the power contracts was a destruction of rights explicitly conferred by the sovereign power of the Province. It was performed without shadow of excuse beyond the fact that the Ontario Hydro needed the money and that the corporations to whom it was payable were outside of the Province. It was the first, and is to this day the most extreme, example in

Canada of repudiation of external obligations effected by the use of the sovereign power of a financially solvent Province. It was the first shot in the interprovincial economic war in Canada. Nobody can be in the least surprised that shells from other Provinces are now exploding in Ontario territory. Mr. Hepburn's and Mr. Roebuck's chickens are coming home to roost—and Mr. Hepburn's is the only shoulder left for them to roost on.

Lorenzo Dutil, *Le Régime de l'électricité dans la Province de Québec. Trust ou Municipalisation?* (Montreal, Les Editions Nouvelles, 1935), pp. 13-15, 65-68. (tr.) Reprinted by permission of the Estate of L. Dutil.

Les Trustards

How did a montrous trust headed by *The Shawinigan Water & Power Company* develop here? Why does this trust charge us such high rates when they could be the lowest in the world? How did this trust and its twins monopolize almost all of our water power . . . ? . . . This company . . . claimed as early as 1926 . . . that it was the fourth largest distributor in the world, with assets of $55,845,962.53 . . . Why, at the end of 1934, nine years later, its assets are $179,073,505.30. . . .

How did all this come about? Read the relevant laws. Do not think that I am mistaken when I say that these companies are a burden on the people. I will prove it. . . . They live off the State. . . .

These two companies control by themselves or have direct or indirect interests in 81 public utility companies. The Shawinigan Water & Power Company owns a large part of the shares of Montreal Light, Heat & Power Consolidated, thus tops the pyramid of companies which monopolize our water power. Our laws have brought this about. . . .

LIST OF COMPANIES WHICH ARE PART OF THE ELECTRICITY TRUST OF THE PROVINCE OF QUEBEC . . .

THE SHAWINIGAN WATER & POWER COMPANY

I. Companies of which it is the sole owner and which it has absorbed:
  a) St. Maurice Power Company Limited,
  b) Laurentide Power Company Limited,
  c) Continental Heat & Light Company,
  d) Portneuf Power Company,
  e) North Shore Power Company,
  f) St. Francis Light & Power Company,
  g) The Sorel Light & Power Company Limited,
  h) Electric Service Corporation,
  i) St. Francis Water Power.

II. Companies which it controls:
  Quebec Power Company which
  a) has absorbed:
    1) Laurentian Power Company Limited,
    2) Kamouraska Hydro Electric Company,
    3) Basin Electric Company
    4) La Corporation d'Energie de Montmagny which controls:
      i) La compagnie Electrique de Montmagny,
      ii) La compagnie Electrique de Bellechasse,
    5) Montmorency Electric Company,
    6) Quebec Light Heat & Power Company,
    7) Quebec Jacques-Cartier Electric Company,
    8) Canadian Electric Light Company,

9) Frontenac Gas Company,
10) Quebec Gas.

III Affiliated companies: . . .

e) MONTREAL LIGHT HEAT & POWER CONSOLIDATED, which is a large shareholder in . . .

Subsidiaries:

1) Montreal Light Heat & Power Company which owns shares in:
   a) Montreal Gas Company, 99%,
   b) Royal Electric Company, 100%
   c) Montreal & St. Lawrence Light & Power Company, 100%,
   d) Imperial Electric Light Company,
   e) Standard Light & Power Company,
   f) Temple Electric Company,
   g) Provincial Light Heat & Power Company, 95%, owner of:
      (1) Canadian Electric Light Co.
   h) Lachine Rapids Hydraulic & Land Co.; Citizens' Light & Power Co., Ltd.

Maurice Duplessis, "Quebec Looks to the Future", *Industrial Canada,* vol. 52, no. 3, July 1951, pp. 85-88. Reprinted by permission of *Industrial Canada.*

The Union Nationale: C.M.A. Means Canadian Manufacturers' Association

DANGER OF PUBLIC APATHY

In Canada, the system of government we want is based on real democracy, that is, the government of the people, by the people and for the people. Unfortunately, some people would like to establish in Canada class rule; verbally they favour democracy but, actually, they are working to establish class rule, an oligarchy, being the government of the people by a certain class, and for a certain class. . . .

To start with, in the Province of Quebec—I do not wish to offend anyone—we have assuredly the best government in the world. You will excuse me if I do not say any more on the subject on account of my humility preventing me from so doing.

SPIRITUAL VALUES COUNT

In our province we deeply believe in fundamentals, one of which is that spiritual values are the necessary bulwark of real and enduring progress. No country can really prosper for long without recognizing, in fact and in practice, the incomparable values of spiritual riches. . . .

FREE ENTERPRISE IN QUEBEC

In Quebec, we believe, because we have common sense, that the government cannot do everything and should not do everything. After all the government is a real manufacturer of a general and unpopular product called taxes, a product concerning which over-production is most inappropriate. Too many people are inclined to ask the government to do everything under the sun, forgetting that what the government gives comes firstly from the people.

In the Province of Quebec, because we believe in human dignity, because we respect the soul, the spirit and mind of mankind, we firmly believe in free and private enterprise, and this policy of ours is not a new policy for us. It was, it is and will be the policy of the present government of Quebec, that is to say it will be the policy of the Province for at least the next forty years. . . .

QUEBEC SOLIDLY CANADIAN

In the Province of Quebec, in short, you do not find exactly Paradise—although the ministers are saints—but in the Province of Quebec you may be sure of one thing: that our traditions are based on loyalty, fidelity, stability, free enterprise, spiritual values, religious and national traditions that are as solid as the Quebec Rock.

C.M.A. means "Canadian Manufacturers' Association." It may also signify "Can Multiply Achievements." "C" stands for "Co-operation," "M" for "Milestone," and "A" for "Achievement." . . .

In thanking Mr. Duplessis at the conclusion of his address to those in attendance at the Annual Dinner, Hugh Crombie, First Vice-President, prefaced his remarks with a few sentences in the French language.

Wilbur Arkinson, "'Voracious Appetite' For Profit Urged Controlled," *Montreal Gazette,* November 5, 1955.

Pure Exploitation

Quebec, Nov. 4—Prime Minister Maurice Duplessis today flatly warned the Quebec pulp & paper industry that "when self-control disappears and is replaced by abuses then state control becomes necessary." It was the strongest warning the Quebec Government leader has ever given the pulp and paper industry. The prime minister said "controls of any kind are distasteful to the Province of Quebec but they become a necessity under certain circumstances."

Mr. Duplessis in his comment did not specifically mention the climbing newsprint prices but it was plain he had these in mind when he discussed the situation at his weekly press conference here today.

It has been reported for some time that Quebec was considering the possibility of a measure of control over the pulp and paper industry but this marks the first time Mr. Duplessis has been so emphatic on this matter.

DUPLESSIS DECRIES SHORTAGE HINTS

Mr. Duplessis also had some caustic comment on what he termed the "trial balloons" launched by R. B. Fowler, president of the Canadian Pulp and Paper Association, who this week hinted there might be a shortage in newsprint.

Mr. Duplessis said the Province of Quebec was the place in Canada and United States where the forestry situation was "the best."

He said this did not mean the situation could not be improved. He said there were certain abuses committed in the past and it could not be expected that these conditions could be remedied in a few years.

"It is certain that in the past 10 years at least the lands and forests situation has improved," Mr. Duplessis declared.

He said "our forests constitute our greatest natural resource because they possess the faculty of renewal. No other natural resource has this faculty."

"The forests," Mr. Duplessis said, "are essential to the water-power of Quebec, a means of fertilizing the soil and serve to prevent floods."

"The forests of Quebec also provide this province with ample fish and game and also serve to provide a good living for thousands and thousands of people," Mr. Duplessis added.

Mr. Duplessis said that if those who sent up trial balloons about the threatened lack of newsprint did so in the hope they could increase the production "to the point of compromising the forests of Quebec they are wrong as far as the Province of Quebec is concerned."

The government leader said the forests of Quebec should be used reasonably and should "not serve as a means of exploiting the public, who, after all, are the real owners of our forest lands."

He reminded the pulp and paper industry that the "forests do not belong to the companies."

COMPANIES ONLY RENT PUBLIC LANDS

"They are simply the lessees of these lands and like any other tenant they should use their leases reasonably," Mr. Duplessis asserted.

"It is evident that the forests of Quebec must not and should not be used to the prejudice of the population of Quebec who are the real owners of this property," said Mr. Duplessis.

Mr. Duplessis said he always was in favour of "legitimate profits" which were essential to the successful operation of any industry or business.

"But abusive profits are nothing but pure exploitation," he added.

He condemned what he termed the "voracious appetites" displayed in certain quarters.

"It is evident that free enterprise and the economic system under which we operate is the most democratic system in existence," the premier declared.

The prime minister said it was "essential that business leaders do nothing to further the arguments of the Socialists and Communists and to harm the free enterprise system in general."

"Self-control has always been the best control but it happens sometimes that when self-control disappears and is replaced by abuses that state control becomes necessary," Mr. Duplessis told the press conference.

"The High Cost of Loving", *Canadian Forum,* vol. XXXV, no. 421, February 1956, p. 241. Reprinted by permission of *Canadian Forum,* copyright 1956.

Quebec Newspapers are Kept Ladies

Premier Duplessis of Quebec has never been one to let his concern for civil liberties interfere with forthright action against unpopular minorities or people who defy his authority. His docile majority in the legislature can be counted on to give his prejudices the status of law. Usually his victims are sufficiently unpopular that his flexible definitions of justice strike a responsive chord in the electorate. The current legislation against the pulp and paper companies takes advantage of the deep-seated sentiment against "foreign" ownership of Quebec industries and rests on a solid foundation of cupidity on the part of newspaper publishers. By virtue of the legislation Quebec newspapers will receive their newsprint at the old price, but like other kept ladies, they will probably find that virtue has nothing to do with it—the baubles were not really for free.

At the time of writing the bill is being revised to correct "mistakes" before the final debate. This scriptural reinterpretation may result in the deletion of some of the objectionable features mentioned below, but it is hard to see how the economic dependence of the press on the goodwill of the government—the plaint of these remarks—can be avoided without jettisoning the bill entirely.

The legislation was brought in after the newsprint companies had ignored Mr. Duplessis' warning that Quebec newspapers must be exempted from the recent price increases. The new bill freezes the price to Quebec consumers for two years at the old level. Having undertaken to control the price, Mr. Duplessis must also control the supply. The companies are required to continue supplying the newspapers with the amount they used in September, 1955, pending the appointment by the government of a four-man newsprint board with power to allocate supplies. The members of the board are to hold office during "good behaviour" (Mr. Duplessis believes that he was elected to govern). The board will have the power to vary the supply of newsprint to any periodical because of changes in circulation or "any other circumstances" and to determine how much of the total Quebec consumption shall be supplied by the various newsprint companies. The decisions of the board cannot be appealed in the courts and no legal action can be taken to delay them.

Lest the power of the government be too circumscribed by specificity, the following blanket provision has been included in the first draft of the bill:

> The lieutenant-governor-in-council, by regulation consistent with the foregoing provisions, may make any suppletive, interpretive or ancillary provision calculated to ensure the fair and effective carrying out thereof.

The irony of this legislation is, of

course, that it is much more dangerous for the newspapers whose interests it is alleged to further than for the pulp and paper companies. The fixed price on the ten percent of their production that is sold within Quebec will not drive any of the companies to the money lenders, nor will the levy to finance the newsprint board distress them unduly. They can feel reasonably sure that the government is not going to use the new powers to jeopardize seriously the province's most important industry. The newspapers, on the other hand, can feel no such assurance about their freedom of expression. Mr. Duplessis has never seemed reluctant to use whatever means were at hand to reward his friends and punish his enemies.

Some observers see hope in the fact that the section of the bill providing for the newsprint board does not come into force until decreed by order-in-council. They infer that Mr. Duplessis is hesitant about taking so drastic a step . . . but how else can he guarantee an adequate supply of newsprint to Quebec newspapers under a fixed price? Regulating the supply by legislative enactment is too rigid to be workable. Allowing discretion to the newsprint companies would give them the same power over the press as the proposed board, and Mr. Duplessis is peculiarly sensitive to the abuse of power by others.

The criticism of the new measure has come mostly from outside Quebec and—if we can judge from past situations involving civil liberties—it will strengthen rather than weaken Mr. Duplessis' following at home. Perhaps the failure of Quebec newspapers (except *Le Devoir*, at the time of writing) to point out the implications of the legislation for their own freedom marks the beginning of a new era of prudence.

"Hon. Maurice Duplessis", *Monetary Times*, vol. 127, no. 3, March 1959, pp. 69-70. Reprinted by permission of the *Monetary Times*.

Hail

Quebec Province's Prime Minister, HON. MAURICE LENOBLET DUPLESSIS, Q.C., has had to be a mining engineer, a financial genius and an economic architect as well as legislator and administrative executive in the course of building Quebec to eminence as an industrial entity renowned for its stability and fine fiscal position.

Actually, Quebec's chief executive, like his father before him, is a lawyer. Born a judge's son in the pulp and paper city of Trois Rivieres in 1890, Maurice Duplessis is a law graduate of Université Laval in Montreal and returned to his home town to practice law. He was elected for the first time as member of the legislative assembly for Trois Rivieres in 1927 and has never been defeated since. Elected leader of the Conservative Party of Quebec in the opposition benches in 1933, he uncovered an early flair for architecture by erecting a Union Nationale coalition out of his own followers and a Liberal splinter group and won the mandate to form a Quebec government in 1936.

LOW PER CAPITA DEBT

Quebec, the largest of Canada's provinces, within three years achieved the lowest per capita debt, with the single exception of the Province of Alberta. The new government also effected sociological reforms in pensions and such matters, and started a vast highway construction program. The Duplessis party lost at the polls in 1939's war hysteria, but returned in 1944 in time to inherit the administration headaches of the postwar cutbacks in the economy.

Since that time, Premier Duplessis has had an uninterrupted opportunity to build the economy of his native province. Quebec has always traditionally been an agricultural community, but a shift in population from rural to urban living indicated drastic changes. Mr. Duplessis stepped up farm credit facilities, placed priorities on electrification of rural areas, and embarked upon extensive roadbuilding activities. Extra emphasis was put upon agricultural education, and assistance was extended through the agronomist services and to farm co-operatives. With these steps, despite lower manpower resources on the farms, agricultural production has actually increased to new peaks, so that Quebec in its new industrial role will continue to be well fed.

TALENT FOR INDUSTRY

Wartime emergency industrial production convinced the Quebec people, predominantly French-speaking, that they really have a talent for industry, and their government at Quebec realized that important steps must be taken to realize such economic ambitions. Quebec's traditionally classical educational system flexibly adapted itself to teach more science, commerce, economics, and the professional studies. The government built a technical and trade schools system that has no equal throughout Canada.

To fill in any gaps in the labor force that the new industrial existence would require, the government co-operated with labor and management as well as municipal groups in forming apprentice training facilities that have handled some 40,000 apprentices between 1946 and 1956. In addition, there are technical schools for paper-making, textiles, mines, graphic arts, furniture making, fisheries, sawmill trades, and 20 agricultural schools.

Already the greatest producer of hydro-electric power, Quebec set out to develop more energy at low cost to attract new industry. Such great existing plants as the Beauharnois development on the St. Lawrence River and several power plants on the St. Maurice and the Gatineau rivers had their capacities stepped up with new turbines added, and the bulldozers and tunnelling crews worked far into the northern bush country to harness new streams, such as the tremendous Bersimis project. As a result, in 1957 Quebec used some 32 billion KWH's of electricity, far exceeding the per capita power consumption of any single country or area in the world, and some three times the consumption of 1939.

TURNS TO GEOLOGY

Something more than people trained to jobs and power for the wheels of industry was necessary, and Premier Duplessis turned to geology for some of the answers. He made important deals with investment capital for the development of Quebec's great mineral resources and encouraged prospectors in many ways to go out and find still new riches in the rock of northern Quebec. The word passed quickly through the mining world, and mining rushes started. His mining policies developed Quebec as an iron ore mining factor, fourth largest in the world last year. In ten years, Quebec will likely be North America's largest iron ore producer. Vast new deposits of copper and nickel ores have been discovered in the far north, and Quebec has now become a great producer of lithium, columbium, titanium, and zinc. Quebec asbestos mines, already producing more than 65 per cent of the free world's supply of this *grey gold*, are spending a collective $100 million in expansion. All the big names of mining, Cyrus Eaton, Hanna, Kennecot, Rio Tinto, U.S. Steel, and many others already have big stakes in Quebec, and the mining development is attracting new industry in its wake, just as Quebec's prime minister had planned it would.

GOOD FINANCIAL RECORD

Stability has been another important ingredient. Sound and consistent province administration has achieved a good financial record, and as the province's solvency steadied, so did its bond market position, so that today Province de Quebec bond issues are snapped up as soon as they are offered and enjoy a good reputation, with investors.

More than $17,625,000,000 in outside capital has been invested in Quebec over the past 14 years, Mr. Duplessis revealed recently.

"I believe that this is the best testimony that the free enterprise system flourishes in Quebec," the Premier said, adding that his government favors free enterprise because, "we believe it is the only democratic system suited to our needs. Socialism, we should remember, is the ante-chamber to Communism." He has repeatedly decried "this trend of relying on the government for everything."

The climate Mr. Duplessis has created has resulted in some thousands of new industries in Quebec in recent years. The measure of increase in 1957 was at least 262 new manufacturing establishments and some 159 additions to existing enterprises and the establishments of Quebec branches.

Quebec today provides *more than half* Canada's newsprint, a quarter of the world's aluminum production, 60 per cent of asbestos production of the free world, 63 per cent of Canada's clothing production, 48 per cent of electrical appliances, 42 per cent of railway rolling stock, 58 per cent of leather footwear, 67 per cent of cotton yarns and cloth, 48 per cent of chemicals in pharmaceuticals, 40 per cent of industrial chemicals, 93 per cent of tobacco, cigars and cigarettes, 52 per cent of synthetic textiles.

NOT RESTING ON LAURELS

Premier Duplessis, however, is far from resting on such laurels. In his austere office in the Parliament Buildings in Quebec, he is busy with projects for still more new railroads into the hinterland, more broad new highways and bridges so that industry as well as holiday visitors can roll more smoothly. New schools are under construction, more grants to the universities planned in addition to the millions already so spent. There are conferences in progress with new groups of financiers ready to invest in Quebec.

This lawyer who has so effectively blueprinted a sound today and a bright tomorrow for his province has remained a bachelor, although he himself once remarked that he considers he has married the Province de Quebec and certainly he has shown parental devotion to his 4,758,000 children, a family that has shown a 17.3 per cent increase since 1951. This alliance with his province is a full time affair for Mr. Duplessis. He is at his office shortly before or after 9 a.m., works steadily until 6.30 or 7 p.m. before returning to his hotel suite. Every few weekends, he tries to get down to his family home at Trois Rivieres to keep his fences mended as the Member for Trois Rivieres. There is little time for vacationing, but he likes to watch hockey and baseball, and his attachment to the latter extends to following the World Series as closely as possible.

Premier Duplessis firmly believes that destiny holds a great future for Quebec, and he is convinced that the course he is charting will give destiny plenty of scope now that the province has such a setting of opportunity for investment and industry, and the limitless horizons needed to capture the imagination of the adventurous.

Miriam Chapin, *Quebec Now*, (Toronto, The Ryerson Press, 1955), pp. 47-48. Reprinted by permission of The Ryerson Press.

Alas, Poor Birthright

Montreal business men occasionally congratulate themselves on Premier Duplessis' success in attracting American investment, which he promises over and over will always be well treated. "It just pours in," they say.

A lot has poured into Ungava, and a lot of Quebec is going to pour out. *The Globe and Mail* of Toronto commented that all Canada was going to get out of that deal was the biggest hole in the ground in North America. By a private bill in Parliament in 1947, and by legislation put through the Quebec Assembly over feeble Liberal protests, the Hollinger Interests, gold producers acquired rights to explore a large district in northeastern Quebec, from which during twenty years they may select a smaller area for mining. The lease is renewable for two more such periods. They may develop mines, build railroads and highways, towns, airstrips, anything needed for their northern empire. Four hundred and twenty million tons of iron ore lie close to the surface. Quebec is to get $100,000 a year after twelve years, and seven per cent of the profits when they begin, but no fixed rate per ton. Under the old mining law, now repealed, it would have been entitled to about $5,000,000 a year for the expected production. The M. A. Hanna Co. of Cleveland, Ohio, major stockholder in National Steel, one of the big three in steel, is joint owner of Hollinger North Shore and Mining. When the first carload or ore was shipped out, down the 360 miles of rail, through the port of Sept Isles, to Philadelphia and the Pennsylvania mills, no representative of the Canadian Government attended the ceremonies. Premier Duplessis and his Cabinet, George Humphrey, U.S. Secretary of the Treasury and former president of the Hanna Co., were there to give their blessing. The Steelworkers' Union organizer, Joe Rankin, told Montreal papers a few weeks later that he had been run out of Knob Lake by the company police, and not allowed to ride back on the railroad.

Of the twenty-six families settled at Knob Lake (renamed Schefferville for the local bishop, but still called Knob Lake) where the mines are, only five are French Canadian. The better paid employees of the railway, the foreman at the mine and on the Sept Isles docks, are nearly all English-speaking. Knob Lake is now one of the nine "closed towns" on the Côte Nord, towns built and run by "foreign" companies.

Paul Bouchard, *L'Administration de la Province de Québec sous les trois gouvernements de Maurice Duplessis*, vol. 1 et 2, (Québec: Organisation de l'union national, s.d.), pp. 63-68, 79-86; 29-33. (tr.)

Progress, not Poverty

The Liberal Party, the party of those who for 40 years sold the Province's natural resources at a dirt cheap price in exchange for free shares and corporate directorships, naturally tries to distort the work of the Union Nationale which has made the new mining regions of Ungava, . . . productive parts of our national patrimony.

A municipal demagogue, as ignorant as he is pretentious, claims that the exploitation of Ungava will only bring the provincial State one cent per ton of mineral. This is false.

Each year, Hollinger will pay $100,000 into the provincial treasury for an annual working permit. This demagogue then indulges in the following infantile calculation: he divides $100,000 by 10,000,000 tons, which yields one cent per ton. . . .

The government of Quebec could not seize by the throat a company that was going to spend $200 million, perhaps even more, before making one cent of profit. Patriotism must not prevent one from being sensible and reasonable. . . .

Hollinger is reproached for having combined with American interests. This reproach has no logical foundation.

Does the reproach come from the socialists of the C.C.F.? It is well-known that Mr. Coldwell is an English socialist immigrant who thinks of his own country first before considering Canada's interests. Moreover, socialists always look unfavourably on any policy which might help the United States to cope with Soviet Russia. . . .

ANNUAL VALUE OF MINERAL PRODUCTION

From 1940 to 1950

Year	Total
1940	$ 86,418,853
1941	99,700,027
1942	104,404,146
1943	101,840,299
1944	90,198,739
	482,562,064
1945	91,570,982
1946	92,213,656
1947	116,042,000
1948	152,285,045
1949	164,212,245
	616,323,928

For a century, our orators, both lay and religious, took pleasure in speaking about the agricultural vocation of the French-Canadian nation, as if it were the only economic activity that Providence had intended for us.

The Union Nationale most certainly wants to conserve the rural base of our nationality, but it is also firmly determined to give us our share in the province's industrial development.

Part IV

Duplessis and Labour or Duplessis Versus Labour?

Duplessis and the Union Nationale party were anti-labour! This widely-held opinion is supported by such a mass of evidence that it seems beyond question. Yet, in the mid 1930's, the Premier's pro-labour stand earned him the criticism of the business establishment. And, statistically at least, membership in labour syndicates increased greatly in his era.

Québec society in the 1930's was the heir to a variety of past events, traditions and ideologies. The rapid economic growth and industrialization of the province had attracted more and more rural inhabitants to the cities. The population shift, caused by the availability of work in factories, an asset in times of prosperity, became a liability after 1929.

Massive unemployment existed and there was a minimum of legislation, federal or provincial, to alleviate this social ill. There were some 625,000 unemployed in Canada in 1935, more than 14% of the labour force. In the same period approximately 1,200,000 Canadians received direct public relief. This social malaise was critical, but unemployment was treated as a political football: Section 92 of the British North America Act defined labour as a provincial responsibility. The outbreak of the Second World War, not legislation, would eventually solve the problem; in 1945 there were but 73,000 unemployed in Canada.

Labour movements in Québec, and throughout Canada, did not receive great popular support in this period. In 1935 the labour force was estimated at 4,402,000. In the same year, union membership was 280, 648. By 1945 the labour force was 4,520, 000; union membership was 711,117.

The growth of the labour movement was retarded not merely by the lack of popular support among labourers, but also by inter-union rivalry. Craft unions competed with employers and industrial unions; national labour groups vied with international, mainly American, unions. In Québec there was a further complication: Catholic syndicates. The denominational orientation of Québec labour groups was further complicated by *nationaliste* overtones. The formation of the first Catholic syndicates dated from the turn of the century, and in 1921 they were given an official structure when the Canadian and Catholic Confederation of Labour was established. This syndicate was often viewed as a thinly disguised 'company union'. Yet, out of this group arose the most radical labour movement in Canada after 1945, and specially after the Asbestos Strike of 1949. In 1961 the confessional character of the syndicate was abandoned and its name was changed to the *Confédération des syndicats nationaux* (CSN).

The prevalent ideologies of Québec during the Duplessis era were also significant factors in provincial labour relations. The political elite and the masses of Québec shared a common defensive political tradition. The French Canadians, more often than not, viewed modification of the *status quo* as a means of restricting their nationality and their rights. The treatment accorded their fellow nationals in other provinces justified this view. State intervention, *per se*, was suspect.

The political elite, labour groups, the business community and citizens generally also shared a common repugnance for communism and socialism. This fear of the *le gauchisme* was used by politicians, provincial and federal, Union Nationale and Liberal, as a political tool in the manipulation of the electorate. While this is particularly true of Québec, it should be noted that it was a norm in other provinces as well. Mitchell Hepburn's labour policies in Ontario did not significantly differ from those of Duplessis in Québec.

Social, economic and political conservatism, fear of change and suspicion of radical ideologies were dominant characteristics of another influential institution in Québec during the Duplessis era: the Holy Roman Catholic Church. It is incorrect to view the Church as a monolithic body; it is not incorrect to characterize its philosophical and theological base as mainly reactionary *vis-à-vis* the social and economic developments of Québec in the 20th century. Church doctrines on social, political and economic matters were instilled in the faithful through active propaganda in Church-sponsored or influenced newspapers and journals, sermons, the educational system which it dominated, and appeals to the theological basis of all life.

The issue of labour in Québec before, during and even after the Duplessis era cannot be considered in a neat little category entitled "labour". Influential political, economic, social and religious ideologies defined the limits of permissible behaviour and thought. In turn, these shaped the day-today relations of labour and business, labour and government, and even labour and labour.

During Duplessis' first term he was accused of favouring labour at the expense of the business community, as is evident in Weston's article on wage controls in Québec. In the next selection, written by Robert Rumilly, an extremely right-wing historian of French Canada, the racist and anti-American currents of Québec are revealed. The responsibility for these biases is a matter of opinion. They certainly existed before and after the Duplessis era. His, and his party's share of this responsibility are moot questions.

Duplessis' views after the war period are indicated in the two readings drawn from the *Montreal Gazette*. Duplessis clearly articulates the anti-international union bias prevalent in the Province of Québec. He also clearly states the *laissez-faire* outlook, or as one wag has called it, *laissez-nous faire*. Miriam Chapin's response to all this is to stress Duplessis' anti-labour bias.

Father Ledit, in the Jesuit-sponsored periodical, *Relations*, underlines a significant feature of labour relations in Québec during the Duplessis era, the very real threat of communism. The textile strike of 1946, led as it was by Kent Rowley and Madeleine Parent-Bjarnsson, alleged to be Communists, raised the hackles of politicians, businessmen and churchmen. Ledit also supports a position held by Duplessis: both labour and business have responsibilities. That this was personally believed in by Duplessis is without doubt; it is equally without doubt that it was a view held by a majority of the citizens of Québec.

L. J. Roger's article from the 'leftist' *Canadian Forum* interprets Duplessis' policies towards labour in a conspiratorial vein. Roger's article does point out the very low wages existing in many industries in Québec, and the government's unwillingness to make employers abide by the laws of the province. Strikes became inevitable, and the inevitable was suppressed and coerced by police action. What should also be noted, but is not mentioned, is that the minimum wage in Québec in 1957 was about the same as that of most other provinces and that the average industrial wage in Québec was lower than in some provinces, but higher than in most of the provinces of Canada.

The excerpt, also from the *Canadian Forum*, on the asbestos strike well illustrates some of Roger's contentions. This labour incident has been raised, or lowered, to the level of a myth. The Duplessis era is sometimes viewed as if the Asbestos Strike was a great watershed: his rise till 1949 and his decline thereon, in spite of the fact that the Union Nationale's majorities in the 1952 and 1956 elections were 44 and 52. The pro and anti-Duplessis positions were certainly polarized by the strike, but on two poles, and not just an anti-Duplessis one. Some of the prophecies of the *Canadian Forum* article, such as the decline of Duplessis, the removal of nationalism as a factor in Québec labour relations, and the reversal of the Church's attitudes on social matters, should be remembered and questioned. Today, twenty years later, there are indeed different attitudes, but that they are of quality rather than degree is not certain.

That the Church was divided in its attitudes towards labour can be seen in the two following articles. The first, "Custos Guards" is drawn from a book of essays on the Asbestos Strike called *La grève de l'amiante*, edited by Pierre Elliott Trudeau. Two points are noteworthy: the mixture of State and Church affairs and the conflicting views within the Church itself. In the next reading, selected from *Relations*, the *nationaliste* and Jesuit publication, the division is evident. It is true that churchmen differed in their views, but it was over ways of procedure and not over basic ideology. Some consideration should also be given to the alternatives suggested by the Church, and especially to a consideration of its anti-Duplessis and Union Nationale facets, if any.

Much of the material presented so far underlines Duplessis' opposition to labour. The last selection indicates statistically the growth of union membership and the wage increases in Québec during the Premier's régimes. The statistics are accurate, but in the wage increases it is well to note the declining purchase power of Canadian currency, something that Bouchard omits to do.

An evaluation of labour as an issue in Québec in the period 1936 to 1959 requires constant inquiry into why Duplessis and his party followed the policies they did, and particularly why he was returned to power if his policies were offensive to such a large sector of the electorate as Labour. It is also necessary to evaluate the alternatives provided by those in opposition to Duplessis, and to ask if they were pro- or anti-Labour. Finally, it is necessary to place labour problems within a national context, not merely a provincial one.

William Weston, "Wage Control Spreads Rapidly in Quebec", *Saturday Night*, vol. 53, no. 47, September 24, 1938, pp. 17-24.

Modernistic Trends in Quebec

Gradually to bring its wage and living standards into line with those in the rest of Canada seems to be the labor policy of the Quebec government. This is one phase of the modernistic trend in Quebec, which became evident when the Duplessis administration came into power in 1936. Other steps include new highways, a provincial power scheme, and rural credits. While such measures seem merely to follow paths already trodden by other provinces, the Quebec government has revealed, on a few matters, a reluctance to follow slow but sure methods, a desire to over-ride obstacles by methods which some critics call autocratic. The task of making over a people who have been schooled to cling to the past can not be easy.

Labor conditions have been of leading concern in the new government's policy because they have been backward. At the same time they have been a difficult subject because much of the industrial development has been on the basis of cheap labor. The government's problem has been to try to raise standards without alienating industry. And that is a dangerous experiment when business conditions are poor. One finds, consequently, regulations which are wide rather than intensive, aiming to give a little help to a large number of people, and to spread the cost over many kinds of industry.

Quebec has the usual kind of legislation for dealing with Labor matters. There is a Quebec Trades Disputes Act, an Industrial Disputes Investigation Act, and other laws dating back several years. The present drive, however, is centred about two measures which have been overhauled by the new administration. One was known as the Collective Labor Agreements Extension Act in earlier years, the title being changed to the Workmen's Wages Act in 1937, and to the Collective Labor Agreements Act in 1938. This law parallels the Industrial Standards acts of some other provinces, empowering the government to extend to all engaged in a certain industry a wage scale which has been agreed upon by a reasonable proportion of its employers and workers. The second is the Fair Wage Act which is the successor to the earlier minimum wage law, both men's and women's occupations being now included.

Soon after the 1936 election, a special committee was appointed to consider amendments to the Collective Labor Agreements Extension Act which had been passed in 1934. The committee held sittings in a number of industrial centres to hear suggestions from representatives of employers' and workers' organizations. Its report to the government resulted in substantial changes in the content as well as in the title of the law.

A collective agreement under the Act means an agreement respecting working conditions made by the representatives of an association of employees on the one hand and, on the other, by the representatives of an association of employers, or by one or more employers. The government has the power to make such an agreement obligatory on all the employers and employees concerned in the district. Thirty days notice are first required for the filing of objections and possible inquiry. The Minister of Labor is instructed to consider if "the provisions of the agreement have acquired a preponderant significance and importance for the establishing of conditions of labor, without serious inconvenience resulting from the competition of outside countries or the other provinces."

Collective agreements have been given the force of law in recent months as follows:

Building trades: Montreal and district; Three Rivers; St. Hyacinthe; Hull; Quebec; Sherbrooke and Drummondville. . . .

Barbers, Hairdressers, etc.: Three Rivers and District; Sherbrooke, Lennoxville and Magog; Farnham, Cowansville, Bedford and Sweetsburg; Valleyfield; Rouyn and Noranda; Hull; Victoriaville; St. Hyacinthe, Drummondville, Granby, Sorel, etc.; Quebec. . . .

In collective agreements many difficulties have been encountered through hasty adoption of ill-considered measures. It is one thing for employers and employees to make a mistake in an agreement concerning themselves, but it is more serious for the government to pass that mistake along in the form of a law to others who were not a voluntary party to it. After a building code had been adopted for Montreal, it was decided to exempt repair jobs amounting to $2,000 or less. The fact that such an exemption was considered necessary to encourage repair work is significant of itself.

If wage controls held up repairs, would they not interfere just as much with new building? A ridiculous confusion resulted from this exemption. Plumbers stated that if they installed a new sink, they would have to charge the code rates, because that was classed as new work. But if they replaced the trap under a kitchen sink, that was a repair job at competitive rates, even though the trap installed was quite new. Consequently, they never were sure just what rate they were earning, nor what rate they should charge the customer. This is an example of the absurdity of detailed regulation of ordinary business.

And in a recent regulation of the barbering trade in Montreal, the government has ruled that the price of a haircut must vary according to the day of the week! It is to be cheapest on Monday or Tuesday, and to advance as the week advances. We surmise that this is on the principle of what the traffic will bear, because there is an assumption that hair cuts, like baths and clean shirts, are in more intensive demand at the end than at the beginning of the week. But we still contend that it defies all logic and disregards all costs. There is no real reason why a haircut should be worth more, or cost more, on a Friday than on a Monday.

The Fair Wage Act, replacing the former minimum wage law, covers all employees who have not availed themselves or who do not desire or are unable legally to avail themselves of a collective agreement. It also applies to cases in which the Fair Wage Board is satisfied that an association of employees cannot agree with an association of employers or with one or more employers contracting personally for the adoption of a collective agreement.

The high hand of government authority is seen in 1938 changes. Now the government has the power to revoke or amend any order under either act. Of course it can not change the collective agreement itself, but there is significance in the fact that while an agreement must first be arrived at before the government can give it effect, there does not have to be agreement between employer and employee to call off the deal. A further change enabling the government to make an order, in regard to either a collective agreement or a mimimum wage, retroactive for a period up to four months may also have drastic effects.

These Quebec measures reveal the dual approach to the wage problem found in most of our provinces—the enforcement throughout an industry of a standard wage schedule as agreed upon between a reasonable proportion of employers and workers, and, in other trades, the adoption of a minimum wage. The first is to put the power of the government at the disposal of groups which are strong enough to do their own bargaining, but which so often find the chiselling employer and the unscrupulous worker so hard to control. The second is for those classes of workers who are too weak to organize, and of course for those employers who seek to take advantage of that weakness.

Under its Fair Wage law the province continued the extensive set of regulations covering women workers, about thirty different industries being under such regulations. The past two years has brought a persistent effort to tighten the regulations and their enforcement, and to include minimum wages for men workers.

One of the most recent orders applies to hospital workers of both sexes. It was estimated that about 7,000 hospital workers in the province would be affected by the order, which dealt with working hours, room and board, and other factors as well as wages, and that about 3,500 of them would immediately receive additional remuneration totalling over $250,000. Of course the joker in this case is that there is no private capitalist to absorb the extra costs; hospital revenues come from patients and from municipal and provincial funds, so that the entire increment to the employees must enter at once into the bills of either the patients or the taxpayers. It affects distribution of wealth, but whether in an advantageous way is at least debatable.

The most far-reaching order of the Fair Wage Board, however, was a blanket regulation issued last December, and which, embracing every class of worker except those specifically exempted, attempted to eliminate sub-normal wages in one grand sweep. It divided all such workers into six major categories, including office workers, school teachers, and many others not commonly reached by minimum wage regulations. It was estimated that nearly 80 per cent of the province's 670,000 workers, including 155,000 women workers, would be affected by the order, and that resulting wage increases would total about $26 millions, or about 5 per cent of the total wages.

This blanket order was subject to some change before it took effect, however. The objections were not so much to the wages specified, as to the other working conditions, which tended to interfere with those controls which are essential to good management. The Canadian

Manufacturers' Association and other organizations claimed that the previous method of inquiry into and regulation of individual lines of business was sounder. It felt that overtime rates for any work beyond 48 hours per week, as proposed in the order, would be both impractical and impossible. It also objected to the power of the Fair Wage Board to control the classification of an employee as intruding on the employer's liberty of action. The order prohibited reduction in the rate of pay of any employee earning up to $200 per month, or the payment to the successor of such employee of a lesser rate than that enjoyed by the employee replaced.

Obviously, this would "freeze" the costs, leaving complete dismissal as the only alternative in a difficult time. The Montreal Board of Trade pointed out that the clause "would prevent the carrying of employees through slack periods at reduced pay, and also the replacement of retiring employees, who have reached their present salaries or wages through years of service and experience, by other persons at a lower rate; it will also interfere with any established system of regular annual increases."

Changes in the order before it was finally made effective were too numerous to be dealt with here; the significant point is that in its original form it showed little regard for the liberty of good management on which the whole future of the province depends, and without which minimum wage regulations will do it no good, because there must first be a job before you can regulate that job.

The Quebec labor policy, along with the industrial standards acts of four other provinces, and the minimum wage regulations of most provinces, illustrate the social tendency of today, which assumes that people can be legislated into good jobs and good wages, and that suppression of profits is feasible and advantageous. The trade union movement, and collective bargaining between well-managed unions and well-managed groups of employers, have on the whole been a good influence on the country. Minimum wage regulations may have protected workers against the small proportion of chiselling employers, but at the same time they have injured the higher grades of workers, so that it is doubtful if any net gain to the average worker has resulted.

The power of law-making by mere administrative act, as exemplified in respect to collective agreements in Quebec and by industrial standards in certain other provinces, is definitely a story of regulation which increases unemployment and relief. A policy which would encourage employment and good wages, by stimulating rather than depressing business activity, would be better for everyone concerned.

Robert Rumilly, *Histoire de la Province de Québec*, vol. XXXVI, (Montreal, Les Éditions Fides, 1967) pp. 119-122. (tr.) Reprinted by permission of Les Éditions Fides.

Jewish-Masonic Influences

The leaders of the large American labour federations built up an enormous power base, lived like feudal lords and warred among themselves. The . . . C.I.O. . . . defied the domination of the American Federation of Labour. Its leader, John L. Lewis, the son of a Welsh miner, had been a gold prospector in Colorado before becoming a strike organizer and union president. A disciple and lieutenant of Samuel Gompers, he wanted to overshadow his chief or to succeed him. The new tsar, a man endowed with the physique and temperament of a brute, who ignored the law, scorned court orders —and rode around in the most recent model Chevrolet—made the oil magnates and the metal kings tremble, and even threatened Ford in his own fief. Then his agents crossed over into Canada. . . .

The international, i.e. American unions, had launched a general offensive in an attempt to monopolize labour organization in Canada. Their agents aroused the latent communist sympathies of the cosmopolitans employed in factories in Northern Ontario and Quebec's Abitibi region. In the Saguenay area, the "nationals", disciples of Mgr. Eugène Lapointe, had anticipated them by secretly organizing the National Syndicate of Aluminum Employees at the end of 1936. The national syndicate submitted a long memorandum to the Aluminum Company of Canada outlining the demands of the Arvida workers. . . . The "internationals", surprised by this move, took the offensive elsewhere. The International Longshoremen's Association demanded supremacy over a national syndicate in the port of Montreal. When the Cunard Company resisted, the International threatened to boycott its ships in American ports. Finally, the International Ladies' Garment Workers' Union affiliated with John L. Lewis' C.I.O., started a strike in the garment industry in Montreal. . . .

In Montreal, the strike paralyzed the dress industry. The international union demanded the signing of a collective agreement eliminating the Catholic Workers League of the needle trade industry. "It is a revolutionary strike", declared Alfred Charpentier, president of the Confederation of Catholic Workers. The strike organizer, Bernard Shane, was an American Jew. It is true that, in the garment industry, the employers were also Jews. In this industry . . . the Jews have become masters "notably of the economic life, but also of the social and professional life". The French-Canadian workers had to choose between two forms of exploitation by the Jews. Nearly all the strike leaders greatly admired republican Spain and greatly opposed the Padlock Law. Abbé Jean Bertrand, the head Chaplain of the catholic syndicates of Montreal, condemned communist infiltration and the actions of professional agitators, and recommended that the American strike leaders be deported. Mgr. Gauthier supported this request. Encouraged by Hepburn's success, Maurice Duplessis and William Tremblay issued a sort of ultimatum to the International Ladies' Garment Workers' Union: a return to work within twenty-four hours and peaceful negotiations. The International refused to comply. Duplessis ordered warrants for the arrest of Raoul Trépanier, president of the Trades and Labour Council, and Bernard Shane, head of the committee organizing the strike.

But the Jewish-Masonic leadership of the international unions remained semi-secret, and these unions recruited quite a few dues-paying members among the French-Canadians in certain industries in Montreal. . . .

Abel Vineberg, "Need For Security Noted By Premier", *Montreal Gazette,* August 8, 1964.

Duplessis on the Solidarity of Employers and Employees

Premier Maurice L. Duplessis told a delegation representative of workers who were employed in war plants, who waited on him at the local government offices with a series of demands, that he was fully cognizant of labor's rights, anxious to protect them, as shown by the record of the two governments he has headed, but, said the Premier, he preferred to deal with recognized labor bodies.

He warned the delegation, headed by Jean Paré, and with Miss Madeleine Parent and Robert Haddow as other speakers, that they were showing the indications of disunity in labor ranks when they ignored their official spokesmen. Where would be the strength and solidarity of organized labor if each branch was to speak to the government on its own behalf? The members of the delegation were members of international unions, said the Premier, and their mouth-piece was the Provincial Federation.

Mr. Paré said that the delegation represented an emergency movement, and was not intended as a reflection on the official labor spokesmen who were to see the Premier shortly.

Mr. Duplessis said that the government he had headed from 1936 to 1939 had been the first in Canada to enact a statute recognizing the right of unionism. He was still of that opinion, but he wished to point out that there could be no employees without employers, that if there was no security and solidarity for employers they would not locate in the province, and since their stake in coming to the province was the greater, as were also obligations on the basis that they have more obligations it followed that there must be a feeling of security. [*sic*]

The Premier referred to an article in an important New York paper which he had read the previous day, and which said that traces of communism could be noted in some of labour's action in this period of reconversion. He did not think that the workmen of Quebec would imperil their present fine reputation of stability, which was their greatest asset, as it was for all the province, and the government certainly would not tolerate subversive movements.

WORKERS HAVE OBLIGATIONS

Workmen in the province should realize they undoubtedly had rights, but what was perhaps more difficult for them to appreciate was that the possession of right[s] involved obligations. The prospects of new industries coming into the province were excellent, the Singer company was adding a five-million dollar plant to their installations at St. Johns, and other prospects were good, but it was necessary that there be stability.

The delegation said there are 45,000 men out of work in Montreal, and advantage was taken of this situation to offer them half of the wage rates they had been getting. A mimimum wage law would help, said Mr. Paré. The Premier said that there was a minimum wage law in the province, thanks to his government. He agreed with the delegation that the matter of jurisdiction as between the province and Ottawa, after having taken wage rates under its control during the war, was not putting through a bill to continue that state of affairs, not, emphasized the Premier, that for the time being he was making any criticism of that or any other government policy.

Mr. Duplessis said that the delegation would have to admit that labour and social laws in this province, while not perfect, were as close to that as could humanly be expected. He was willing to listen to suggestions for betterments, and had proved that last year when the Labour Relations Act had been amended at the request of labour, but, repeated the Premier, let labour not disturb the difficult reconversion period with injustices to employers and their own province. There was a right to strike, and there was also abuse of that right.

He promised the government would do all that was possible for labour, but preferred that the official representatives of labour come to him.

"Sense in Pay is Duplessis Idea," *Montreal Gazette,* February 23, 1949.

Tinker Capitalism

Quebec, Feb. 22.—(CP)—Premier Duplessis said today a man failing to do an honest day's work is a "traitor to his family, his province and his country."

The Quebec Government Leader made the statement to the Legislative Assembly during discussion of the salaries of Government employees. He said it was time for a "return to common sense" in consideration of social questions.

Premier Duplessis said in the past there had been "atrocious abuses" in employers' dealings with their employees but "most of that has been remedied."

He said if Quebeckers want to benefit from the province's "immense natural resources" they must start by convincing themselves of the necessity of work.

"There is a lot of natural talent in the province but let us make it bear fruit," he said.

Premier Duplessis said that due to "loafing on the job," a building supposed to cost $800,000 costs more than $1,000,000 today.

He said a Northern Quebec bishop had come to him "almost in tears" because of the excessive cost of a hospital building that had been started.

"Leaders tell labourers not to lay more than 300 brick[s] a day," he said. "If the farmer had the same mentality I don't know where we would be."

Premier Duplessis called for a return to old ideas of work and told the House of the case of a tinsmith in his home-town of Three Rivers, Que., who repaired the Duplessis' kitchen stove, fixed chairs, did odd jobs and was worth $75,000 when he died.

"There's nothing like that today," said the Premier.

Premier Duplessis said that provincial civil servants who number 15,000 have received pay increases totalling $4,000,000 to $4,500,000 a year.

All have insurance whose costs are paid for by the Government.

"They work scarcely 6½ hours a day and if they work an hour extra they get $1 for it," said the Premier.

The Legislative Assembly passed the $3,098,650 budget for the Provincial Secretary's department and the $18,528, 400 budget for education.

Miriam Chapin, *Quebec Now*, (Toronto, The Ryerson Press, 1955), pp. 54-59. Reprinted by permission of The Ryerson Press.

If the Premier were Married

The Catholic Syndicates (CTCC, *Conféderation de Travail Canadien et Catholique*) are by far the liveliest outfit in the labour field. They claim over 100,000 members, though these may include a few chaplains, some foremen, and perhaps a few who hold cards in other federations. Their main strength is outside Montreal, in the textile mills of the eastern townships, the asbestos mines, the pulp and paper mills of the Saguenay, the aluminum works at Arvida, and in some of the building trades. In 1922, they first put their federation together out of a few scattered locals. The Church was obviously uneasy about the growing power of the Internationals, the unions of the Trades and Labour Congress (most of them affiliated to the A.F. of L.) and the Canadian Congress of Labour ones, linked with the C.I.O. The Jesuits were active in organizing the Syndicates. Their constitution calls for co-operation between capital and labour. In their early years their leaders were picked for them, and their chaplains had a veto power in their executives.

For a long time they were little better than glorified company unions. The boss would give the local organizer a donation for the annual picnic and he would sign on the dotted line. As late as 1942 a Syndicate local was used, with the fervent guidance of a Montreal priest, to break an A.F. of L. strike at Arvida. Visits to the wives, devotion to the parish, anti-semitism, appeals to nationalism, did the job. But with the election—a genuine election—of Gerard Picard as president in 1946 and Jean Marchand as secretary in the following year, a change that had been moving under the surface came into the open. The memory of the depression in the 30's, the general organizational drive of the war years, the activity of the Internationals cutting into their membership, the anti-conscription feeling, the quarrels with the Duplessis Government, all served to force a more active policy. Nowadays the Syndicates fight like wildcats, in strikes and politics.

Picard is a man so thin and desiscated-looking, with such black circles under his keen blue eyes, that he hardly looks as if he had strength for a day's work. Yet he holds his Federation together, is acquainted with the most remote locals, sees hundreds of people in a week and is pleasant but decisive with all of them, flies off to Europe to represent Canada at an international meeting or two, makes clear and emphatic if not eloquent speeches in his staccato, rasping voice, carries on involved negotiations, and presides over turbulent meetings with skill and authority. Nor does he quail before the frequently experienced wrath of the Premier. Jean Marchand is a different type; a product of Dominican Father Georges Lévesque's training at Laval, he is a handsome genial young man, an intellectual of great charm, a remarkable orator. Indeed he could be called an authentic spellbinder. These two, with Phillippe Girard, an older man who came up from the ranks of the tramway workers, and Réné Rocque, now inactive, welded a mass of inexperienced, low-paid, often semi-illiterate people into a genuine union.

Their hardest trial of strength came in 1949 in the asbestos strike against the Johns-Manville Company. Msgr. Charbonneau supported them—to his ruin—and their chaplain, Father Camirand, stood with them. They won, not only a better wage contract, but a measure of protection against the killing dust. At a press conference Premier Duplessis flung out the remark that the priest was *écervelé* (brainless), and the Syndicates made effective use of that in their propaganda. For they must have the aid of the Church, even though each year they take unto themselves more independence. One of their leaders, in private conversation, commented that they are not strong enough to stand without the Church, and he added softly, "Yet." Their present situation was well summed up by Rodolphe Hamel, of the asbestos union, when he said they got along all right with their employers—"it seems to be always the Government we're in trouble with." . . .

This move toward co-operation is the most interesting development in the labour field since the war. They got together primarily to fight Bills 19 and 20, passed by the 1954 Assembly. These bills were actually sections of a Labour Code, which the Premier proposed five years before, and which was halted by protests from all quarters. He has since been enacting it piecemeal. Bill 19 provides that a union may be refused certification or decertified if it "tolerates, among its organizers or officers, one or more persons adhering to a Communist party or movement." Originally "doctrine" was added to this, but opposition of the Superior Labour Council, an advisory body in which the Church is represented, brought about deletion of that word. Since the bill is retroactive to 1944, it seems that a union could be decertified if it had once had someone whom the Government chose to call Communist on its staff. The decision in such cases is left entirely to the Labour Relations Board, and cannot be appealed to the courts. Minister of Labour Barrette said the bill was needed because the Supreme Court of Canada had decreed in a Nova Scotia case that a union could not be refused recognition (certification) because one of its officers was a member of the Labour-Progressive Party (Communist). Labour leaders who complain that the bill does not define "Communist" are told by Mr. Barrette that no definition is needed. Bill 20 was apparently directed especially at the Montreal Teachers' Alliance. It provides, under the Public Services Employees' Disputes Act, that a union forbidden under that act to strike, shall lose its certificate if it "orders, declares, or encourages" a strike, or if its leaders do so. This bill also is retroactive to 1944, so that it covers the 1948 teachers' strike in Montreal. *Le Devoir* says that if the Premier were married, and had only daughters, he would make the oldest a son, retroactively. . . .

The Federation of Labour (A.F. of L.), stands aside from any such action. These Trades and Labour Congress unions seem to think they can get more by co-operating with National Union, presenting polite requests and gaining minor concessions. Yet the groundswell of feeling in the rank and file is so strong that Roger Provost, President of the Federation, felt it imperative at the 1954 convention to deny accusations of "softness," and to make a violent attack against both Federal and Provincial Governments, which was warmly applauded. He said Ottawa had broken its promises to Canadian workers, made at the end of the war, and that it was neglecting the problem of unemployment. He said the Provincial Government has caused the right of association to disappear from the Quebec scene. He denounced Bills 19 and 20, saying that the unions had been the first to clean their ranks of subversives, but that they believed the way to combat subversive ideas was to give the workers the liberty and security they deserve. And he opposed the retroactivity clauses, saying, "to make laws in a spirit of revenge against individuals is unwholesome and unworthy of a statesman." No comment from the Premier.

Joseph-H. Ledit, s.j., "Les leçons d'une grève", *Relations,* no. 70, October 1946, pp. 312-314. (tr.) Reprinted by permission of *Relations.*

Communism is Intrinsically Perverse

Last September 9, after a strike that had lasted since early June, the textile workers of Valleyfield returned to work at Montreal Cottons. "Madeleine Parent" told them that they had won a "striking" success. In reality, not one of the conditions that the workers had set at the beginning of the strike was accepted by the company. Success went altogether to the employers on the one hand, and to Mr. Rowley and Mrs. Bjarnsson on the other. The workers are footing the bill with their foregone wages of more than 275,000 work days. During this time, they accumulated debts everywhere, which they must now pay. They spent the hot summer days picketing and fighting. Their comrades in Montreal, who went on strike at the same time as themselves, had returned to work by July. This had been part of the over-all strategy of the strike organizers. The workers of Valleyfield, more docile *vis-à-vis* the organizers than those of Montreal, endured until disaster struck. Let us not deceive ourselves! Messrs. Gordon and Aird have interests other than the Montreal Cottons' factory. Mr. Rowley and Mrs. Parent-Bjarnsson consider Valleyfield as a little corner in the great class struggle, and everyone will speak of the workers with sobs in their throats and tears in their eyes. All in all, the workers of Valleyfield are paying in misery, hunger, and ill-feelings that will perhaps take years to overcome. . . .

On 23 September, 1942, Mr. Kent Rowley was released from the internment camp where he had been sent in June 1940, and discovered that he had become a model of patriotism. At this time, the communists were crying out as loudly as they could against Quebec, which people in high places felt was not patriotic enough. The influential people thought that a dose of communism could not help but do good in our province. Rowley was smart enough not to become a member of the Labour Progressive Party. Without any formal affiliation, he gave himself a lot of elbow room. He immediately started to organize the textile workers, in Valleyfield as well as in Montreal, within the United Textile Workers of the American Federation of Labour: local 100 in Valleyfield and local 102 in Montreal.

He found a situation made to order, especially in Valleyfield. The resentment which the workers harboured against the company was almost indescribable. Undoubtedly, the war had somewhat improved working conditions; not too long before the workers had been paid paltry salaries. To be sure, they worked all day long, but the Company only counted the time when the looms were functioning usefully,—that is to say, it deducted the innumerable daily work stoppages. Discontented workers were forced to leave the factory and, in reality, the city, for it was the only factory in Valleyfield. The Catholic Syndicates had attempted to organize something to protect the workers. Forced to use only honest methods, they ran up against the omnipotence of the Company and had to . . . desist. We have not met a single person who has spoken of Colonel W. G. E. Aird with respect or sympathy. Either this ex-military man is incapable of collaborating with the local population, the Company's public relation service is inoperative, or the Company regards its workers with the utmost indifference as long as its dividends continue. This Colonel has painted a true picture of himself, we believe, in what he wrote to Mr. Rowley, on 29 January 1943:

> I hope you realize that this Company has a very definite idea of its responsibilities towards its employees, the government and the public. Flowing from this sense of its responsibilities, we have a realistic concept of our duties in the situation provoked by your activities and your organizational methods.

This was a declaration of war—something which Mr. Rowley enjoys more than anything else in the world. Released from the internment camp on 23 September, he felt that he was already far enough advanced by December 23 to offer himself as negotiator to the Company, whose reply we know. Not until February did he obtain letters patent for local 100; the same month, he requested the creation of a conciliation and inquiry commission.

At the time he claimed that 1,800 workers had chosen him as their representative. With Madeleine Parent, he had circulated a petition to this effect; to be sure, 508 names were not even on the Company's pay-roll, and several signatures had obviously been written by the same hand. These details did not embarrass the organizers who knew that the petition, passed from door to door, had been a superb propaganda *coup*. When the Company rejected this argument, the Rowley-Parent team had admission cards signed; they obtained 1,432 such cards which they then submitted to the commission of inquiry. To examine these cards, the Minister of Labour appointed an official inspector, Mr. Bertrand Rose, c.r., who decided in favour of the local. The commission of inquiry and conciliation, although recognizing that the local had not furnished valid legal proof, still rules (by a majority) against the Company. Decisions; appeals. The final word was given on 13 June, 1944, by the National Labour Council in Ottawa: the Union had not proven that it represented the workers, no more so at Valleyfield than at Montreal. Was anything more needed to enable our comrades to demonstrate to the textile workers that Capital and Government had joined forces in order to oppress them? . . .

Kent Rowley and Madeleine Parent claim that they are not communists. Perhaps they are not officially. Why commit the enormous *faux-pas* of declaring oneself a communist in the Province of Quebec when all the organization work remains to be done? The tactics of Rowley and Parent conform perfectly to what the *Tribune* and the *Province* preach. Let us say . . . that if these two agitators are not communists, they follow and implement the party line in the province of Quebec. And they disrupt the working population wherever they work. . . .

From this moment on, agitation became chronic. In June there was a strike in Montreal as well as in Valleyfield. In Montreal it lasted until the second half of July, when the workers had to capitulate. The Company demanded that negotiators other than the Parent-Rowley team be appointed; the latter took refuge in their last bastion, Valleyfield.

Here, the strike was illegal from beginning to end. Picketing, violence. The mayor ordered the municipal police not to intervene. On 13 August, there was a riot, brought under control by tear gas bombs thrown by the provincial police. The city lived under a regime of violence. The clergy were insulted in the streets. The windows of workers who were not sympathetic were broken; suppliers who would not extend credit to the strikers were threatened with the same fate; Mr. Aird's house was damaged; paving-stones which were ripped up from the streets were used to cause damage or to threaten people. Finally, on August 25, Rowley and Beaucage were arrested, not for illegal labour activities but for acts of violence. The witnesses to the charge were numerous. More recently, Madeleine Parent was also apprehended (under the name of Mrs. Bjarnsson) and was accused of having given $20 to children so that they would change their testimony. All that these two agitators can do now is to pose as martyrs of the working class.

After the workers had returned to work in Valleyfield on September 9, they held a vote to notify the Company of which labour organization was instructed to negotiate for them. By a huge majority they chose local 101 of the U.T.W.A. Thus, these brave people entrusted their fate to two persons accused of public crimes and who, if they are not officially communists, faithfully follow the "party line".

On Wednesday, 11 September, the communists held a meeting at Samson Stadium in Montreal, a meeting that had been publicized by thousands of invitation-circulars. All in all 150 people came. If we deduct the curious, few people remain. The imminent danger of war and the textile strike were spoken of—these two things being linked together in the party line. The secretary of the *Jeunesses ouvrières progressistes* club, Gabrielle Desjardins, announced that the Young Communists (the first time, since it was banished in 1940, that this expression was used in public in Montreal) was going to join with the *J.O.C.* and other Catholic organizations. Let us not laugh too much at this youthful cry in an empty hall. Valleyfield has demonstrated that two agitators can work up the feelings of the people in one of the best small towns of this province.

Let us take the opportunity to expand on these events and to make the following remarks of a more general nature:

1—The companies—When a company opens a factory, especially in a small town . . . where it is the only company providing work, it does not merely create an instrument of production; it assumes social responsibilities *vis-à-vis* the worker who leaves his land or who comes from elsewhere to work in the factory. Such a worker will henceforth be a permanent resident; he will have permanent relations with his butcher, his grocer, his landlord and his doctor. The factory owes him stability. Now this can only arise if there is co-operation between the factory and the local population.

This co-operation cannot be unilateral. It is all very well for a manager to say that he is aware of his responsibilities and that he will do what he wants, but this is paternalism or dictatorship. He can surround himself with foremen who will tell him that the local population is bizarre and must be handled with firmness; he can also put the local politicians in his pocket, as has happened in more than one place. This attitude can only result in conflict.

The necessary condition for success is a state of good feeling between the company and the local population. The company must finally understand that the latter is to a very great extent French-Canadian and Catholic. It is thus ridiculous to hire a managing staff which is [not only] almost entirely non-French-Canadian, but Freemason, as sometimes occurs. On the other hand, the company has much to gain by drawing its foremen and industrial relations agents, the aristocracy of its factory, from the local population. These intermediaries will provide the link between the company and its workers. . . .

It is in the company's interest to reach an understanding with the national Catholic syndicates, whose head office is in Quebec; the latter do not receive orders from foreigners to stop work or to start a strike. They are certainly in no way affiliated with Moscow. They ask no more than to arrive at an understanding. As they are a small organization and do not have the huge resources of the large unions at their disposal, it is easier to reason with them; by their very nature, they favour conciliation. If the companies want to drive their workers into the hands of such agitators as Mr. Rowley and Miss Parent, all they have to do is war against the national Catholic syndicates. It may annoy a Protestant or a Freemason to have to do business with Catholics, but *Business is business.*

2—The Government—One of the striking things about this affair is that the law has not been applied. The Padlock Law is directed against communists. Sometimes it is observed, sometimes not. Several strikes were declared illegal. No measures were taken against those who committed acts recognized to be illegal. Mr. Rowley, Mr. Beaucage and Mrs. Parent-Bjarnsson were arrested not for violation of labour legislation, but for breaches of the common law. . . .

The Government must not only be above quarrels between citizens. Its impartiality must be obvious to all. The majesty of sovereign authority requires this. For a party to accept money or favours from a private organization, and not to intervene because of electoral considerations, inevitably leads to the debasement of public authority, and thus to anarchy and revolution. Integrity is as indispensable to the politician as to the magistrate. The distinction between technical legality and justice must disappear, and legality must be upheld. When one parleys with revolution, one has already capitulated. Pity the country which only yields to force; the force of money, electoral force, the force of bullies on the picket line. Over and above force a law of justice must reign.

3—The workers—Where the national Catholic syndicates are established, you might say that the game is almost won. We have little sympathy for those thick-headed industrialists who refuse to recognize this obvious truth. As they only believe in their own force, let them now bend before the revolutionary force which crushes them in their turn! Where the companies have been intelligent enough to collaborate with the local syndicates, Christian ones dedicated to conciliation, there will occasionally be clashes and foolish acts; but sooner or later these conflicts will be settled.

Where these syndicates do not exist, our Catholic workers will almost inevitably be organized into neutral unions. In the latter, there are apt to be leaders who are communists or who have communist tendencies. In this case, it is indispensable that our workers be organized in addition into confessional groups. For many years, the Holy See has requested this of them. Since these organizations cannot aim directly at union activity,—inasmuch as union activity is in the hands of a neutral or foreign leadership—these Catholic organizations must be conceived of differently. . . .

In Canada, it seems, our *J.O.C.* and *L.O.C.* have a magnificent field of action open to them in the factories where Catholic syndicates have not been organized. Pius XI sent them here to conquer the infidels or those who are in danger of so becoming:

> If this mission, which they must carry out in the mines, the factories, and the dockyards, wherever people work, sometimes requires great self-denial, they will remember that the world's Saviour set the example, not only of work, but also of sacrifice. (*Divini Redemptoris,* p. 70)

Everyone, especially our brave family in Valleyfield, might well recall the words of Pius XI:

> Communism is intrinsically perverse, and on no grounds can anyone who wants to save Christian civilization collaborate with it.

L. J. Rogers, "Duplessis and Labor", *Canadian Forum,* vol. 27, no. 321, October 1947, pp. 151-152.

Duplessis' Tricks

One of the most important prejudices in the mind of Quebec's nationalist Maurice Duplessis is his deep-rooted hatred of international labor unions. If the Quebec premier had his way, these "outside" labor organizations, whether of the AF of L, the CIO or the railway brotherhoods, would be banned in Quebec, and replaced by locally controlled unions of the Catholic Syndicate type. As long as federal wartime labor regulations were in effect, Premier Duplessis did not feel free to commence his "anti-foreign union" crusade—but judging by recent indications, this crusade will be announced any day now. Ever since March, when Ottawa stepped out of the labor scene, organized labor has been the victim of a war of nerves in Quebec, and the blitzkreig stage may be reached at any time.

Premier Duplessis does not feel bound by any laws which he himself has not placed on the statute books. The existing Quebec Labor Relations Act of 1944, which was put through as one of the measures of the Godbout regime, is not treated as provincial law by either Duplessis" Labor department or his Attorney-General's department. This law provides, among other things, that an employer is required to negotiate for an agreement with the representatives of the employees' association of which the majority of his employees are members. For a time, the Duplessis technique was to grant certifications to unions representing a majority of the employees, but to do nothing further to persuade the employer to bargain in good faith with the certified union, even though this is the clear intention of the Act. Of late, the process of sabotaging the Act hes been carried a step further—now applications for certification from legitimate unions are frequently held up in the Labor department for months, seemingly to give company unions an opportunity to intimidate or bribe the employees of the plant into leaving the legitimate union. When this process has been successful, the Department calls for a plant election, on short notice.

Another trick has been to grant certifications, then revoke them without warning and with no other justification than the claim of the employer that the union "no longer represents the majority of his employees." This device has been employed in several Quebec strikes, generally at the time when union strength had reached its lowest point after weeks or months on the picket line.

The system of "collective decrees," peculiar to Quebec labor law, by which wage scales for an industry are set at three-way conferences of employers, government and labor, is currently being used as a weapon against legitimate unions. Decrees granting wage increases to all workers in the boot and shoe industry of Quebec—except those belonging to the

AF of L Boot and Shoe Workers Union—were recently issued. True, the increases were very small, but the effect of the decrees was to penalize those workers who belong to a legitimate union.

The latest move against "outside" unions reported as being considered by Premier Duplessis is an amendment to the Labor Act which would require union organizers to be licensed by the department. Like most of his other anti-labor moves, this step is taken ostensibly against the Communists in the labor movement—but past events have indicated that the Quebec Premier believes at heart that every union is Communist which is not a company union or a unit of the Catholic Syndicate group.

So far, Duplessis has shown his hand most strongly against organized labor in plants and industries controlled by Quebec capital. Industries controlled by "outside" capital, with which the Premier is presumably not on such familiar terms, are shown no particular favors by the Quebec Labor department—and organized labor in such plants is given good service by the department.

To see how Quebec labor law works for a "native" employer with good political connections, let's take a look at the story of Local 313 of the United Rubber Workers union (CIO-CCL), at the Chambly plants of Bennett's Ltd. Early in 1946, organizer Jack Lerette went into Chambly to organize the 300 workers at the two Bennett plants, and within a matter of weeks he had a solid membership built among the French-speaking workers there. Organization was not difficult, because the Bennett workers were being deplorably underpaid and, into the bargain, tyrannized by a feudalistic absentee management. Wages averaged little better than $20 a week for experienced men doing fifty hours of skilled work, and some men received as low as $14.50 for a week's work—after deductions by the company for water and light charges in the company-owned houses of this little company town. Added to that, the company refused to tell the employees how their wages were calculated, what their hourly rate and hours of work amounted to, or what deductions were made. Not until the union took legal action against the Bennett management was this practice halted, almost a year later.

When a majority had been signed into the union, application for certification was made by Local 313, and after a fairly lengthy delay the certification was granted on May 11, 1946. When the Bennett management refused to bargain in good faith with the local, the Quebec Labor department appointed a conciliation officer, early in July, 1946. This officer, unprovided with any particular rights or powers, failed to accomplish much. He was, in fact, unable to get the Bennett management to agree to any of the clauses of a standard union contract. Even then, the Quebec Labor department took no action to direct the company to bargain in good faith, as required by the Act. Instead, at the recommendation of the conciliator, an impartial arbitration board was set up, as provided by the Act in cases of last resort.

When the board was finally established after months of tedious delay, in November, 1946, it was composed of one representative of the union, one of company and one of government. Before it began its sessions, the management was asked if it would agree that the findings of the board should be binding on both parties. True to form, Bennett's management refused to agree to this. Instead of calling off the whole procedure, now made meaningless, the board solemnly held hearings at intervals throughout the winter. Then on March 30, 1947, it issued a unanimous recommendation calling upon the company to sign a collective agreement with Local 313 without further delay and to grant a wage increase of ten cents an hour to its employees.

This recommendation was unanimous—signed and approved by the company's representative on the board—but Bennett's management still refused to bargain in good faith or even to discuss the matter with representatives of Local 313. The only course left for the union was strike action—and the strike was called on April 15, 1947—something over a year after the date when the Bennett employees first sought the help of the Quebec Labor department in getting the collective bargaining agreement promised them by the Quebec Labor Act.

This strike was a legal one in every respect—the union having wasted more than a year of time and considerable money in complying with the provincial labor regulations. Yet the Labor department took no action then, and has taken no action to this day—after almost five months on strike—to direct the company to comply with the law of the land.

Instead, the company was provided with the services of one hundred provincial police almost from the beginning of the strike to enable it to convey strikebreakers through the picket lines thrown up by the three hundred strikers. Backed by this costly show of strength, the company combined intimidation and bribery in an effort to get the workers to break the strike ranks—but almost entirely without success. The Quebec courts, presumably after consultation with the Attorney-General of the province, granted the company no less than thirty-five injunctions against strikers and union officials forbidding them to picket the plant, or even to watch from a distance of a block or more.

This treatment was given to a union holding a legal strike—a union whose leadership has always been known as non-Communist both in Canada and the United States. At the time this is written the company still refuses to meet with the union, in spite of several union offers, and in spite of the fact that plant production is far below normal both in quantity and quality. The morale of the strikers, backed by contributions totalling more than $60,000 from other URWA locals and the international office, is still high. The rubber workers intend to fight this strike out to the finish—to find out once and for all whether legitimate organized labor has any legal rights in the province of Quebec.

"Asbestos Strike", *Canadian Forum,* vol. XXIX, no. 341, June 1949, pp. 51-52. Reprinted by permission of *Canadian Forum,* copyright 1949.

Asbestos: Strike or Revolution?

Five thousand asbestos miners in Quebec have been on strike now for over three months. That strike is not only an unprecedented event in Quebec: it is one of the most dramatic struggles in the history of Canadian labor, and its social, economic, and political implications are certainly of national, if not international, significance. Yet it has received scant attention in the Canadian press outside Quebec.

On February 13 the 2,100 workers of the Johns-Manville plant at Asbestos went on strike. They were soon joined by the 2,500 workers of the Bell Asbestos Company at Thetford Mines. The Quebec Labor Board revoked the certificate of the union and declared the strike illegal because the dispute had not been submitted to arbitration. Immediately the Johns-Manville Company called upon the government to protect its property, and Duplessis sent in a hundred and fifty provincial police. On February 21 the Asbestos town council formally protested that the police had been drunk and disorderly, had "committed in streets," and had "u the employees . . . of provoking trouble. In March the company charged the strikers with dynamiting a company railroad and kidnapping a mine official, but the local people claimed the police created those incidents. The police are said to be receiving an extra $50 a week from the company: a set-up which *Le Devoir* terms "a lease-lend of the provincial police to Johns-Manville."

For twelve weeks the strikers conducted themselves with extreme propriety, refraining from picketing because that would be illegal, and attending church each day to pray for the granting of their demands. Then early in May the "most gentlemanly" strike ever seen in Canada erupted overnight into one of the most violent. The trigger that set it off was the rumour that Johns-Manville was bringing in strike-breakers. Road barriers were thrown up and all cars coming into the town were stopped. Seventy-five carloads of police were rushed in, and the Riot Act invoked. Violence died down, and a week later fifteen strike leaders were arrested.

The Catholic Union of Asbestos Workers is affiliated with the Canadian Catholic Confederation of Labor, which has generally been regarded as far from militant in its collective-bargaining tactics, and as reluctant to strike if it could be avoided. The union was demanding union security through the Rand formula, wage increases of fifteen cents an hour (to raise the basic wage from eighty-five cents to one dollar), and better control of the deadly asbestos dust. Negotiations had been under way at least six weeks before the strike started. The general council of Catholic Syndicates set up a $100,000 fund to aid the strikers.

In March the three major labour consses, the CCT, the TLC, and the Catholic Syndicates, met in joint conference to combat Duplessis' anti-labor program, and issued a statement of support for the strike on behalf of the 250,000 organized workers in the province: an unprecedented display of labour unity.

Even more surprising is the attitude of the Catholic Church, which has heretofore frowned on strikes. The parish priest, Father Philip Camirand, who is the union padré and has veto powers over union decisions, declared: "If I were a miner I would be on strike". The Catholic Sacredotal Commission of Social Studies, a group known as the "Modernists", who believe that the Papal Encyclicals on Social Justice should be interpreted literally, called on all Catholics to aid the strikers through church collections. Representatives of the Duplessis government are said to have appealed to the Canadian Papal Delegate, Ildebrando Antoniutti, to intervene, but if so, the appeal was unsuccessful. At the height of the riots, the Archbishops of Quebec and Montreal asked that strike collections be taken on Sundays in all churches until further notice.

Politically, too, the strike has tremendous significance. The Catholic Syndicates used to form the backbone of Duplessis' support, but now they are bitterly opposed to him and his whole anti-labour program. In the coming federal election that feeling will no doubt express itself against the Progressive-Conservatives, with their Union Nationale alliance. (An interesting sidelight is that Ivan Sabourin, the leader of the Progressive-Conservatives in Quebec, is the legal adviser of Johns-Manville.) Since Drew's bid for power depends upon substantial gains in Quebec, this might well be the deciding factor in the election.

Whatever the outcome, the asbestos strike is certain to have far-reaching effects. The change in the social pattern of Quebec, the weakening of the barriers between French and English trade unionists, and the shifting political alignments will make themselves felt throughout Canada, and the reversal of the Catholic Church's position on economic issues may well be felt far beyond our national boundaries.

Pierre Elliott Trudeau, ed., *La Grève de l'Amiante*, (Montreal, Editions Cité Libre, 1956), pp. 407-409. (tr.) Reprinted by permission of the Author.

Custos Guards

This mimeographed work of 184 pages bears no date, but it was first circulated in December 1949. On the front page, the following title appears: "Collections of documents—*On the Asbestos Strike* (1949) organized by the Confederation of Christian Workers of Canada—for the exclusive use of Messrs. the members of the clergy."

No author's name is mentioned; but at the bottom of the last page, instead of a signature, the latin word *Custos* (guardian) is used to designate the individual, or group of individuals, who gathered the documents (which are for the most part authentic . . .) and who generously interlarded them with defamations and warnings directed against certain members of the clergy (in both the upper and lower hierarchy), against the leaders of C.C.W.C., and, for good measure, against third parties.

As a result of certain "indiscretions," the work circulated somewhat beyond the exclusive circle of "Messrs. the members of the clergy," and soon became known as "the Custos Report." Various attempts to identify the author have been made, and the most interesting was discussed in . . . *Le Travail* (G. Picard, 2 March, 1951 and 16 March, 1951); but he did not arrive at anything conclusive. . . .

The report, reputed to have been brought to the attention of Rome both by ministers in the Duplessis government and members of the Quebec episcopate, was followed in mid-February 1950 by the resignation "for health reasons," of Mgr. Charbonneau, Archbishop of Montreal.

Any speculation as to a causal link between these two events is futile; furthermore, it would be an insult to the intelligence of the Vatican administration to believe that it might be influenced by such a biased dossier. But it is still clear that the Custos Report was devised by one group of Catholics as a weapon of war against another group of Catholics who held different social conceptions.

Because we do not believe that anonymous information and secret reports are likely to create that climate of tolerance and frankness which prevents political and social differences from degenerating into religious vendettas, we do not have any scruples about violating the "confidential" character of the Custos Report. And because this report is deeply indicative of the type of arguments which official Quebec thought uses against "leftists" (others would say "conservatives" against "progressives"), we publish below large extracts that we ironically preface with the phrase that Custos inscribes at the beginning of his study (p. 6): "In short, it is simply a collection of documents upon which we have commented with all the objectivity possible for someone gripped with emotion before the scandalous behaviour of certain people."

There are probably secret leaders and several other categories of people responsible (for the strike); let us make it clear that we are not accusing, *a priori,* the Christian union leaders and the chaplains involved in this affair, of being agents of Moscow. But . . . (to the) query: did this strike suit Moscow's purposes, we answer with a peremptory yes. . . .

In this way Custos establishes his thesis: anyone implicated in the strike was either an unconscious instrument of Moscow, or one of its perfidious agents. No one is above suspicion for, according to Custos, "the permanent doctrine of the Comintern" teaches, among other things that

Catholic syndicates must be infiltrated by communist agents who, camouflaged as good Catholics, should attempt to assume the leadership.

But where did Custos learn about "the permanent doctrine of the Cominterm"? In statements by Lenin which have been badly digested and taken as dogma. The following, for example: "Syndicates are truly the schools of communism". . . .

And above all in the so-called teachings of Canadian communist leaders Custos states that he learned about these teachings through "stenographic notes taken during a course on tactics" by a communist who has since been converted. Now, without a doubt these "notes" were wholly fabricated either by Custos or by an imbecile who duped Custos magnificently. These pages, cited in their entirety, would constitute a lasting monument to the stupidity of the "right," but a few paragraphs will suffice.

Let us listen to how (according to Custos) Mr. Fred Rose, a communist leader and a Member of Parliament to boot, speaks to militant communists, bragging about the grandeur of the encyclicals, lauding the virtue of those who apply them, contending against the spiritual direction of the confessional, mocking broad-minded persons, speaking ironically about the "dear" syndicalists and finally only recognizing communist material among the ignorant or naive priests and among the proud, ambitious and opportunist!

If it is relatively easy to diffuse our ideas in socialist and liberal workers' groups already won over to the Communist Party, it was not so when we began our propaganda among the Catholic proletariat. The social teaching of the Pope is what we should fear most for it permits the resolution of the social problem without revolution, and thus without the disorder which alone enables us to take power, to exterminate our adversaries and to expropriate their property which is indispensable if we are to continue the revolution. But the social solution proposed in the encyclicals cannot bring the workers happiness unless it is achieved on the basis of a perfect Christianity. It requires from the two antagonists, the employers and the workers, self-sacrifice, the abandonment of their excessive ambitions, an upright conscience, absolute loyalty and perfect charity, . . .

"La liberté syndicale", *Relations*, no. 198, June 1957, pp. 141-142. (tr.) Reprinted by permission of *Relations.*

The Church Dissents

While our bishops declared that "Legislation on the right of association . . . must be continually improved in order to prevent abuses by those who, under one pretext or another, do not understand the need for healthy syndicalism and the rôle of order and social peace that it is called upon to play" (Lettre collective des évêques du Québec sur *le Problème ouvrier* en regard de la doctrine sociale de l'Eglise, 1950, n. 174.), the actual position of labour freedom in Quebec has continually deteriorated since 1944.

First, there was the unjust law of 1946 which deprived a large section of teachers of their incontestable right to arbitration. The law had already denied them the right to strike. Both these acts struck a mortal blow to the prestige of the teaching profession and the fair payment of those persons engaged in it. Then, both before and after the failure of the attempt to domesticate syndicalism by the infamous "Labour Law," unfortunate and repeated experiences in factories before the Labour Relations Commission and even the Courts soon pointed to the conclusion that "if the workers cannot freely negotiate with their employers collective agreements which protect their legitimate interests, if they do not have the legal means to guard against bad faith in negotiations, then their right of association is illusory. (*ibid.*, n.176). As early as 1950, our bishops declared . . .: "Union freedom must be recognized in practice, notably through effective sanctions set by the law concerning dismissals or pressures exercised because of union activities." (*ibid.*, n.177).

Since then, no improvements have been effected; on the contrary. Today, it appears that, all too often, intervention by the Ministry of Labour combines with the calculated or illogical decisions of the Labour Relations Commission practically to banish union freedom in many geographic and industrial sectors of the province, and to unduly protect labour organizations (usually of a foreign allegiance, as in Baie Comeau and Shawinigan regions), whose only distinctive attribute is a malleable political nature. The just doctrine in this area has, however, been clearly formulated: "The executive authority of the State must not intervene . . . in problems of labour relations, except when absolutely necessary, for example to help re-establish an equilibrium disrupted by the dominance of those who possess too much economic power." (*Le Problème ouvrier*, n. 177).

Conclusion: . . . in Quebec, unions appear to be but the expression of the powerful and of friends of the régime. As regards union representation, the former take the lead in spite of the opposition of management, legal manoeuvres and occasionally police force; the latter, after being held back by shady means, are imposed by law (as in the case of the Montreal taxes). But between these two minority groups, there is the huge mass of wage-earners who hunger for and thirst after justice. Their salaries are not sufficient to meet the demands arising from their responsibilities as heads of modern families; the unjust disparity in their working conditions is a factor contributing to social imbalance. They possess the prescriptive right to choose that labour organization which enables them to obtain justice for themselves and peace for society. "Can any man, and above all any priest and any Christian, remain deaf to the innermost cry of the masses who, in the world of a just God, cry out for justice and fraternity?" (Pius XII).

Our provincial State, like all the others, thus has "the duty to protect this right and to help put it into practice." The genuine freedoms need to be cultivated and protected for the fundamental reason associated with the eminent dignity of the human being and with the brotherhood of man. . . . We would be prouder of our province if all the basic freedoms flourished here, especially the effective freedom of the less privileged to group themselves into unions of their choice, which would be true freedom of association. . . .

Paul Bouchard, *L'Administration de la Province de Quebec*, vol. III, pp. 71-77; 83. (tr.)

Primacy of Human Capital

As soon as it returned to power, the Union Nationale amended the Labour Relations Act so as to make it more democratic.

The Liberals had set at 60% the majority needed by a union to be granted certification.

Under the Union Nationale, once a union has organized 50% plus one of the employees in an enterprise, it has the right to certification.

Labour's power of negotiation has thus been greatly increased, and it is quite correct to state that this amendment was the starting point for the remarkable growth of unionism evident in the province since 1945.

. . . The Liberals claim that the Union Nationale hindered the spread of unionism in the province. This is obviously a lie. . . .

Moreover, the official statistics of the Federal Government demonstate beyond the shadow of a doubt that union membership has increased considerably under the Union Nationale. . . .

[See Table 1, p 104]

We will now see, by a study of the activities of the Conciliation and Arbitration Service, that under the

> *Union Nationale,* there were more labour unions, fewer strikes and fewer strikers.
>
> *Liberal Régime*, there were fewer unions, fewer union members, and twice as many strikes and strikers. . . .

From 1940 to 1944, there were 82 conciliation cases in 4 years under the Liberal Régime; from 1945 to 1951, 6 years under the Union Nationale, there were 1,823 conciliation cases. . . .

It is thanks to the leader of the Union Nationale that the minimum hourly wage in the asbestos industry has increased considerably . . .

. . . the asbestos workers received an increase of 25 cents per hour or $12.00 per week . . .

By comparing this minimum wage of $1.25 with that of $0.44 per hour under the Liberal Régime, we must conclude that the minimum wage in the asbestos industry almost tripled under the Union Nationale. . . .

[See Table 2, p 104]

Anyone who studies the labour and social legislation of the Union Nationale in an impartial manner cannot but conclude that it made every effort to assure the primacy of human capital over money capital and to give the workers their fair share in the profits of enterprise.

TABLE 1

NUMBER OF UNIONS

Liberal Régime	Year 1944	(January)	number of unions 673
Union Nationale	Year 1950	(January)	number of unions 965

An increase of 43% under the Union Nationale.

NUMBER OF UNION MEMBERS

Liberal Régime	Year 1944	(January)	number of union members 175,993
Union Nationale	Year 1950	(January)	number of union members 239,800

An increase of 34% under the Union Nationale.

TABLE 2

HOURLY RATES IN 1945 AND 1951

Industry	Wages 1945	Wages 1951	Increase	
Mining	$0.69	$1.23	$0.54	78%
Aluminum	0.76	1.41	0.65	85%
Pulp and Paper	0.69	1.40	0.71	103%
Asbestos	0.62	1.43	0.81	130%

Part V

Duplessis and the Church: Render unto Caesar

Duplessis was a professing Catholic, as were most of the citizens of Québec. The Holy Roman Catholic Church dominated Québec. Although the first of these statements is true, it does not lead, *ipso facto*, to the second. That the Church was one of the dominant ideological and institutional forces during the Duplessis years cannot be denied. However, that the Church abused its theological, moral, educational and social rôles is both a matter of fact and a matter of opinion.

When considering Duplessis and the Church, the question of what properly belongs to God and what properly belongs to Caesar must be squarely faced. Church-State relations in Québec, at least those concerning education, were not based on the separation of powers. To the contrary, section 93 of the B.N.A. Act specifically joined them. The linking of the State and denominational education was designed to protect the rights of the English Protestant minority of Québec. Denominational education, while no doubt approved by the Catholic Church, came about because of the Anglo-Protestants.

In some ways the Church in Québec fulfilled many rôles assumed by the State in other provinces. Catholic hospitals were staffed mainly by nurses supplied by female religious orders. Insane asylums, poor houses, old age homes and other charitable institutions were both staffed and financed by the Church.

In Québec the Church was also one of the prime depositories of French Canadian linguistic, cultural and national interests. For many years this institution had provided intellectual leadership; it had also provided the professional élite of the secular society. Doctors, lawyers, businessmen and politicians were trained and educated in Church-sponsored and supported schools. Catholic doctrine, be it ultramontane or gallican, saw little or no dichotomy in life: morality and politics, morality and economic life, morality and education, and morality and social action were all tightly woven threads in the tapestry of French Canadian society.

In this section of readings we witness complex confrontations. Inasmuch as the Church was a part of the whole society, a consideration of the Church results in a consideration of the many facets of churchmen's actions and doctrines, political, economic, religious and social.

The use by the State of its powers of repression in the name of religion and politics is not merely noted by Rumilly, but approved. Rumilly claims that a significant group in Montreal society opposed the use of public facilities for purposes of communist propaganda and that the Mayor of the city was responding to a majority view. If this be true, and it probably was, it raises the question of democratic oppression, or to put another way, the limits of a minority group's freedom when it conflicts with the views of a majority.

Rumilly emphasized religion and politics. In the next two selections the confrontation is between religious beliefs, with civil rights as an issue, and the judicial powers of the State represented by the Attorney-General of Quebec, Maurice Duplessis, and the Supreme Court of Canada as another. Sandwell, a liberal English Canadian journalist, both approves of and decries the behaviour of French Canadian society and government. The best known confrontation between the Roman Catholics of Quebec and the Jehovah's Witnesses revolved about the personage of Frank Roncarelli, mentioned in the Sandwell article. The Roncarelli Affair was eventually brought before the Supreme Court of Canada. This tribunal awarded Roncarelli $33,123.00 plus interest as compensation for his losses. *Relations*, the Jesuit sponsored review, did not approve of the Court's interference. The response of the citizens of Québec was to take up a public subscription to pay the fine imposed on the Attorney General and Premier of the Province, Maurice Duplessis.

Another *cause célèbre* involving the Church of Québec during the Duplessis era was the Charbonneau Affair. In this instance the confrontation was not between dissenting sects, ethnic groups or ideologies such as communism, but between members of the hierarchy of the Church and important political and labour figures. The catalyst of the affair was the Asbestos Strike whose background was considered in the last section. Cardinal Charbonneau was sympathetic to the cause of the striking workers. He permitted the churches under his care to take up a public subscription to assist the labourers financially. In this policy he was opposed by more conservative churchmen, and he raised the ire of Union Nationale politicians.

An issue such as the Charbonneau affair well illustrates the immersion of the Church in secular matters. The Cardinal was challenged not because he was involved, but because he supported, in the opinion of some, the wrong side. Renaude Lapointe, presently an editorialist at *La Presse*, does not question the Church's right to intervene in secular matters, nor does the article extracted from *Relations*, although their positions, to say the least, differ. In Quebec, it was not the rôle of the Church, but some of its policies, which society questioned.

The selection from *Time*, partially answered in the reading from *Relations*, represents an 'outsider's' view of Church-State relations in Québec. It raises, however, a significant issue: was the State using the Church? the Church using the State? or were the interests complementary so that the purposes of both institutions were served?

The last two selections illustrate brutally the power of the Church and the power of the State. The late T. D. Bouchard had had an illustrious political career. For many years he had been the progressive mayor of his native city, St. Hyacinthe. During the Taschereau and Godbout régimes, he had served in the cabinet, and after the nationalization of some hydro-electric companies during the war, was named president of the State-owned body. Bouchard was also a member of the Senate of Canada. His political ideology was *rouge*, that is, a left wing liberal. He was also anti-clerical, at least to the extent of drawing a clear line between the affairs of God and the affairs of man. He was not a radical but rather a free thinker. His ideological tendencies were never very popular in Québec. On June 21, 1944, he gave his country, Canada, and his countrymen, English as well as French, a history lesson.

In this section we have witnessed confrontations concerning the rôle of the Church in Québec society during Duplessis' regimes. We have not considered the non-confrontation situations, the day to day activities of the Church which were carried out in the shadows of obscurity rather than the limelight of publicity. Nor have we drawn a clear distinction between anti-clericalism and anti-catholicism, but there is a difference and it should be remembered. Regardless of the issue, it must be accepted that the *Québecois* viewed the Church as a functional part of Québec society and not as an atrophied institution.

Robert Rumilly, *Histoire de la Province de Québec*, vol. XXXVI, (Montréal, Les Editions Fides, 1967) pp. 210-212. (tr.) Reprinted by permission of Les Editions Fides.

Freedom of Speech is not Freedom to Slander

The Spanish Civil War was the catalyst provoking or precipitating the grouping of the forces of the "left" in the province of Quebec. Information of an official and unchallengeable nature nevertheless reached Canada . . . *L'Action Nationale* and *Le Devoir* published a letter in which forty-eight Spanish archbishops and bishops, appealing to their colleagues around the world, described the communist atrocities:

We declare that in the history of the Western peoples, we know of no similiar phenomenon of collective madness, nor of a similar number of offences committed, in a few weeks, against the fundamental laws of God, society and the human person. . . .

The number of priests who have been assassinated, from among the secular clergy, alone amounts to about 6,000. They hunted them with dogs; they pursued them in the mountains; they sought them with a passion in all their hiding places. Most of the time they were executed at once and without trial, for no other reason than that they were priests. . . . It is estimated that more than three hundred thousand civilians have been assassinated solely because of their political and, above all, their religious ideas. There is hardly a single village where the most obvious rightist elements have not been eliminated without charges, without proof, and most of the time without trial.

Many had their limbs cut off or were horribly mutilated before they were killed; their eyes were put out, their tongues cut, they were disemboweled, burned or buried alive, killed with axes. . . . The modesty of women was not respected, not even of those who, by their vows, had dedicated their lives to God. Temples and cemeteries were desecrated. . . .

The reaction of the clergy, and of the mere faithful, is easy to imagine. A communist meeting was supposed to be held at the Mount Royal Arena on 22 October. The students of the University of Montreal requested Mayor Raynault to forbid it. According to the lawyers consulted, the municipal council could only forbid such a meeting if they feared a riot. The students then spoke of possible riots. Mayor Raynault forbade the meeting. A social outcast, Hubert Désaulniers, vainly protested in the name of the Canadian Society for the Rights of Man, [a society] that he had just founded with R. L. Calder, Jean-Charles Harvey, Edmond Turcotte and a few others. The *A.C.J.C.* and most national societies congratulated the mayor. Mgr. Gauthier highly approved of the prohibition. He regretted that only the students had protested to City Hall, "whereas in a Catholic city such as this, at least 4 or 5 thousand men should have approached the municipal authorities and made known their will with respect to communist propaganda." . . . Cardinal Villeneuve, in a speech delivered in the Quebec Coliseum . . . also highly praised Mayor Raynault's intervention, and advocated the same means in the war against communism: "The freedom of speech is not the freedom to slander our social outlook, the freedom to insult our traditions, our customs and our religion." Mgr. Decelles of Saint-Hyacinthe was also convinced of the communist threat. The episcopate wanted rigorous measures capable of curtailing communist propaganda.

B. K. Sandwell, "Why French Canada 'Hates' Witnesses of Jehovah," *Saturday Night,* vol. 62, no. 17, December 28, 1946, p. 6. Reprinted by permission of *Saturday Night.*

Why French Canada "Hates"

The root cause of the trouble about the Witnesses of Jehovah in the province of Quebec is that the French Canadians have always believed that they were entitled to be protected against efforts to proselytize among them by any non-Catholic religious or any anti-religious movement.

It is important to remember that in the early days of the British administration of Quebec the ruling authorities adopted a deliberate policy looking to the wholesale conversion of the French population to the tenets of the Church of England, through control and vigorous use of the educational institutions. It did not take the British long to learn that this effort was doomed to failure, and London abandoned it probably a generation before the English-speaking element in the colony (who of course were not the real source of power or holders of responsibility) gave it up also. After that the Quebec majority were never disturbed by anything except the missionary enterprises of private societies, and even these soon ceased to have the backing of the more conservative Protestant churches.

FURIOUS RIOTING

The visit to Quebec and Montreal of Gavazzi, an Italian ex-priest, in 1853 had little support from influential Protestants, but led to furious rioting in both cities. In the nine decades that have followed those events, the Salvation Army has at intervals felt called upon to dispute the religious supremacy of the Pope in French in public places in different parts of the province, and has run into a good deal of trouble in so doing; but hardly anybody else, and most of the time not even the Salvation Army, has undertaken to preach Protestant doctrines on the streets except in exclusively English-speaking areas.

It is quite fair to say that to the French Canadians the idea of religious liberty includes the idea of not being subjected to the persuasive efforts of other religious bodies, of any kind, to induce them to depart from their faith. This is the underlying assumption of the only letters which we have seen in the Quebec press supporting the policy of Mr. Duplessis regarding the Witnesses. The difficulty is to make this idea compatible with the concept of individual liberty as generally entertained in democratic countries, which certainly includes the right to proclaim one's religious ideas pretty widely, though within limitations imposed by the fact that one must not become a nuisance.

The Witnesses, like a good many other earnest fanatics, are entirely unbothered by any scruples about becoming a nuisance, and have unquestionably become one, in practice if not in law, in a good many parts of North America other than Quebec. Like the Communists, the other present objects of the "burning hate" of that province, they were restrained during the war because of their violent opposition to military service, and indeed to any other exercise of the civil power except such as suits their purposes; the Communists ceased to be opposed to service as soon as Russia found herself at war with Germany, while the Witnesses remained as much so as ever in real belief though they eventually accommodated their public teachings to the changed conditions of the times. As soon as the wartime restraints were lifted the Witnesses went to work with tremendous energy, and their distinct craving for martyrdom made Quebec a most attractive place for their efforts. The majority of French Canadians think that there should be some means by which the province of Quebec could stop them, and appear unconcerned as to whether those means are within the law or not. The majority of English-speaking Canadians are disposed to insist upon legality.

The criminal law is in the hands of the Dominion, and has not as yet defined sedition in such a way that there would be much hope of convicting the Witnesses on that charge. Mr. Duplessis holds that the recent pamphlet on the "burning hate" is so denunciatory of the character of the provincial government and the influences which predominate in it that this document is seditious if nothing else is; but he has not yet got any court to render such a decision, and in no other province is there any sign of a disposition to prosecute it. Meanwhile the Witnesses are being subjected to wholesale proceedings under laws forbidding the peddling of literature without a license (most of the Witness literature is offered for sale) and the distributing of handbills and circulars in public places, and there seems to be an attempt to wear down the few lawyers whom they have at their disposal by a series of successive postponements. Last week's decision by the Recorder of Quebec City was on the charge of creating a disturbance.

LEGALLY WRONG

These things would probably have caused little excitement even among Protestant lovers of liberty in Quebec, if Mr. Duplessis had not conceived the idea of preventing the enormous number of Witnesses who are being prosecuted from getting bail, by using his power as Attorney-General to take away the restaurant license held by Frank Roncarelli, the wealthiest member of the sect in the province, and the habitual provider of bail for arrested Witnesses. Mr. Roncarelli has undoubtedly provided a great deal of bail for a great many persons, but the idea that there was anything wrong with that had never been put forward before. The bail is set by the courts, in accordance with their judgment as to what is most likely to aid the course of justice, and it seemed as though Mr. Duplessis was setting out in his capacity as Attorney-General to prevent that which the courts had authorized from becoming effective.

The further observation of Mr. Duplessis, that to continue Mr. Roncarelli's license would make the government a participant and abettor in the crime ot sedition, obviously involved a pre-judgement to the effect that the Witnesses were guilty of sedition, whereas the whole theory of bail is based upon the democratic and British doctrine that an accused person is not guilty until convicted.

The curious thing about the whole business is that the Witnesses are certainly making a considerable number of converts among the French-speaking population of Quebec—as for that matter are also the Communists, the other form of revolt against ecclesiastical discipline which the general mass of French Canadian opinion also wants to suppress by police measures. If the Church of England or the United Church of Canada were to adopt the same missionary methods as these two bodies employ among the French population, the reaction of general French Canadian opinion would be exactly the same; but they do not. The reason for the difference is clear enough. . . .

The Witnesses and the Communists . . . do not have to get along with the Roman Catholics. They cannot do so anyhow. The Communists expect to effect eventually a revolution which will suppress the Catholic Church and probably also all the other churches— including those to which some of the Communists appear at present to belong. What the Witnesses expect is a little hard to determine, but at one time their doctrine included an early Second Coming of the Lord in which they would be rapt up to heaven and their enemies cast into the pit of everlasting fire. "Millions now living will never die."

THEIR ATTITUDE

Protestants, and in the main English-speaking Roman Catholics, in Canada are apt to rely on their own personal efforts for the maintaining of their faith against the efforts of other kinds of believers to subvert it. In English-speaking North America the Witnesses have got into trouble with the authorities and with the public (and they have done so with both quite extensively, to the great benefit of their martyrdom complex) by reason of their attitude towards certain civil regulations, such as saluting flags and singing patriotic hymns in schools, rather than by their propagandism, which there is a general disposition to tolerate as the great majority of other propagandisms are tolerated. The nuisance laws have been invoked against them often, but they are extremely ingenious at remaining within them while continuing to do what the laws were intended to prevent.

It is difficult to make a law that will prohibit a Witness from ringing doorbells to offer literature and not prohibit a brush salesman from doing the same with brushes; yet the two operations are radically different both in motive and in social character. Similarly it is hard to prohibit a Witness from addressing a street meeting and not prohibit a Duplessis politician from doing the same. The French Canadian does not object to the Duplessis politician nor regard him as an enemy of the established order; he objects to the Witnesses and Communists and does regard them as enemies of the established order. But he is having a hard job finding a law that will draw the distinction that he desires.

"La Cour suprême et les Témoins de Jéhovah," *Relations*, no. 154, October 1953, p. 286. (tr.) Reprinted by permission of *Relations*.

The Court Supreme

The recent judgment of the Supreme Court of Canada, which leaves the Jehovah's Witnesses completely free to distribute their circulars with impunity, has taken many people by surprise. The declaration that the freedom of religion must be equal for all is just if this refers to the fundamental freedom to worship and serve God within one's home or in churches and temples. The public worship of a cult should not be forbidden so long as it does not transgress upon the general populace. If it does so transgress, the religious freedom which they demand may degenerate into pure licence. Thus, freedom does not justify the aggressive and disrespectful proselytism of the Jehovah's Witnesses, two examples of which follow:

> In reality, it is the priests of Quebec who upset the peace in this province by stirring up the mobs and the public authorities in order to incite them to act unjustly against the Jehovah's Witnesses. The priests are disturbed because the truth of the Bible exposes them as "the inventors of evil thoughts and of errors", and they fear the back-lash when honest Catholics discover that they have been duped.

And further on in the same publication:

> The conduct of the Catholic clergy does not follow the footpath of the Bible, but rather resembles that of the Pharisees. Catholic doctrine does not follow the route traced by the teachings of the Bible, but rather resembles the pagan dogmas of olden times.

When public worship by one cult does not transgress upon another religious group, it is clear that this cult has the right to expand without restriction. But, when it does so transgress, neither individuals nor the civil authorities, charged with the commonweal, can remain indifferent. That is why the judgment of the Supreme Court astounds us. In cases of this kind, the Supreme Court should only be concerned with examining whether the basic rights, such as the right to build a place of worship and the right to worship, are protected. It is quite normal that the provincial and municipal authorities should satisfy the legitimate desires of the majority so long as the essential rights of the minority are not encroached upon. This point is beyond question. Jurists must find a solution that respects religious freedom and at the same time guarantees peace and order.

Renaude Lapointe, *L'Histoire bouleversante de Mgr. Charbonneau,* (Montreal: Editions du Jour, 1962), pp. 16-17; 19; 63-65. (tr.) Reprinted by permission of the Author.

Duplessis and the Reactionary Clergy

"He was the banderilla in the Bull's neck . . .
He was the thorn in the Cow's flank . . ."

The Bull was M. Duplessis who had sworn to ruin him (Charbonneau).

The slow-moving Cows were the group of reactionary bishops of that day, grouped under the confessionalist, nationalist, ruralist banner of Mgr. Courchesne, the archbishop of Rimouski, who saw himself as the saviour of the threatened Canadian Church. . . .

The Premier, who had already sent several men of the cloth as emissaries to Rome, this time at the beginning of the Holy Year, . . . delegated his own ministers . . . The Minister of Labour and the under-secretary of State for extraordinary Affairs, Mgr. Tardini, had previously corresponded. The latter had undertaken to compile a . . . dossier to transmit to Pope Pius XII and also to arrange an interview with His Holiness.

After they had piously bowed down before Saint Peter's tomb, and paid their respects to the Pope, Mr. Duplessis' ambassadors were invited to participate in a fraternal reunion at the Canadian College with the archbishops and bishops who were in Rome on that occasion.

During the same month, a 184 page report on the asbestos strike, "for the exclusive use of Messrs the members of the clergy" and signed with the latin word *Custos* (guardian) had been circulated in clerical circles in Quebec and Rome and had created a propitious atmosphere. This report, supposedly written by a group of militant Catholics and brought to the Vatican's attention, insinuated that the strike had suited Moscow's purposes. It also accused Mgr Charbonneau and a few others, without naming them, of in effect "becoming accomplices of the communist leaders by exercising an undue influence in an attempt to destroy the authority of the only Catholic government in North America."

Finally, Mgr. Courchesne himself went to Rome to present a long memorandum of 128 pages in which he asked for the heads of Mgr. Charbonneau and a few other people. The former was, although not formally, accused "of no longer agreeing with the hierarchy, of creating a schism in the Church of Quebec by parting company with the bishops and by attempting to divide their support, and of preaching a social progressive, that is to say, leftist Catholicism.". . .

An English Canadian raised in Quebec cannot help but think differently from those raised in other provinces, and a French Canadian raised outside of Quebec cannot completely resemble those who have never lived outside its borders.

This was one of the main reasons why Mgr. Charbonneau, a native of Ontario, differed from most of his colleagues within the Quebec episcopate. He came from the other side of the *reservation* and believed in a peaceful co-existence of the various ethnic groups in christian charity, without, however, abdicating his faith, his patriotism or his attachment to French culture.

His diocese of Montreal was immense, heterogeneous, cosmopolitan and held one third of the province's population. He wanted to take initiatives here which necessarily differed from those taken in other dioceses, something which many bishops would not accept at all.

"I have one million proletarians in my territory, yet I am asked to maintain the rural mentality of those who direct the rural dioceses. They want my *gros bonhomme* to wear the breeches of their *petit bonhomme* . . . They don't see that things will explode . . . and that evolution is preferable to revolution," Mgr. Charbonneau always said. . . .

Leading the extreme right of the episcopate, Mgr. Georges Courchesne, the archbishop of Rimouski, bluntly repudiated the new attitudes advocated by Mgr. Charbonneau and never missed an opportunity . . . to use bitter polemics, especially on the question of making the co-operatives and the unions non-confessional, a principle which he violently opposed. . . .

A man who supported ruralism and conservatism, and who opposed progress, the archbishop of Rimouski was very rigid in doctrinal matters. An intellectual, he read widely, and kept himself well-informed on so-called modern theological errors, as well on the Catholic social movement. . . . A member of the ultramontane school, he opposed progress, was convinced of his moral probity and judged others as deviates and even traitors. According to several people, Mgr. Courchesne annoyed all the other bishops and considered himself the saviour of the Canadian Church and guardian of the doctrine. One day he went so far as to say of Mgr. Charbonneau: "I wonder if this man truly believes . . ."

In the realm of politics, Mgr. Courchesne was firmly convinced that "the more things change, the more they stay the same", and that another leader could do no better than M. Duplessis. It is reported, however, that he actively advised M. Duplessis during the asbestos strike.

"Son Exc. Mgr. Joseph Charbonneau," *Relations*, no. 111, March 1950, pp. 57-58. (tr.) Reprinted by permission of *Relations*.

Charbonneau Resigns

Last February 11, the Holy Father, complying with his request, relieved His Exc. Mgr. Joseph Charbonneau of his duties as head of the archdiocese of Montreal. Ten years of incessant labour in the most populous, motley, and trying diocese in Canada had exhausted the nerves of a man whose health still outwardly appeared robust.

As if the faithful were not suffering enough, press agencies and radio stations, acutely short of head-lines, spread the most fantastic and despicable gossip. . . .

The most wide-spread rumour tended to discredit the social spirit of this man who, as archbishop of a commercial and industrial metropolis in which workers formed the largest part of his flock, had boldly sided with the striking workers in the Asbestos affair. However, the *Civilta Cattolica,* a review published by the Society of Jesus under Vatican supervision, had already published a long and detailed report by a Canadian correspondent in its December issue. In this issue, the charity of Our Lords the Bishops was praised and the very words cited which Mgr. Charbonneau had pronounced in the house of God, words which made the floors shake.

The Vatican published a formal denial, first in the *Ensign* and then in the New York Times Service: ". . . the rôle that he played, far from being criticized, was highly praised."

The widely-read magazine, *Time,* was impudent enough to suggest, mentioning the name of the Apostolic delegate, Mgr. Antoniutti, that Mgr. Charbonneau had been asked to change his attitude on the labour question. Once again, a reply was not long in coming. The very night that the Canadian edition appeared on the newsstands, *Time* suffered a slap in the face. In a telegram addressed to the magazine and to the B.U.P. and P.C. press agencies, the Apostolic delegate "categorically denied that he had ever asked Mgr. Charbonneau to *draw back from his pro-labour stand* and that, on the contrary, he had always approved of and encouraged his very charitable attitude towards all the victims of war, strikes and social injustice."

The spirit of social justice animating Mgr. Charbonneau was drawn from a deeply felt sense of charity. His door was always open. He gave his time and strength without hesitation. He listened to the humble complaints rising from the overpopulated quarters of his city . . . he wanted houses for the families of all his workers, and sun, fresh air and space for all his children. . . .

In all honesty, the *Ensign* could end an enthusiastic editorial with these simple words: "A great priest has made a great contribution. . . ."

Poor peoples, Polish orphans, refugees, workers to whom he preached not to shirk on the job, employers whom he taught not to cheat on salaries and working conditions, the faithful of all different races and cultures whose unity in Christ he held to his heart, . . . priests in his former diocese . . . today all these people are realizing the void left by his departure.

More Sociological than Theological

A controversy, more sociological than theological, has disturbed the Roman Catholic Church in Quebec. The dispute springs from a historical process—the fact that the province is steadily becoming less rural and pastoral, more urban and industrialized.

How shall the church adapt its leadership to the changing society? One faction, led by Laval University's dean of social sciences, the Very Rev. Georges-Henri ("Jolly Monk") Lévesque, argues for a militant championship of the working class, has promoted cooperatives and Catholic trade unions. An opposing group, supported by Quebec's Premier Maurice Duplessis, believes the church must strengthen the rural parishes and stay aloof from class antagonisms, though it should fight for social justice.

These clashing points of view were summed up by an impartial churchman: "It is a question of emphasis. One faction says that we must teach people how to say their prayers, but we must also see that they have good working conditions and have a just deal. The other faction says that if you emphasize the working conditions and the just deal too much, you're tackling a problem which will never be entirely solved, and people may forget how to say their prayers. If you fight Communism, which talks about a heaven on earth, just by saying you can provide better toilets than the Communists, you're conceding the Communists' premise; and you're forgetting the essential point of Catholicism, which is that although we may try to improve this life we must also remember that there is a life beyond."

Last week *Maclean's* magazine, in an article by Ottawa Editor Blair Fraser, brought the argument into the open. Author Fraser gave unstinted support to the Lévesque faction and belabored the opposing group. "The Duplessis government," he charged, " has used every kind of pressure on Laval University to fire [Lévesque]; ultra-conservatives in the Quebec clergy have twice carried their war against him to the Vatican itself . . ." To force the issue at Laval, continued Fraser, Duplessis had withheld half of a provincial $4,000,000 grant.

"Why this concentrated assault?" asked Fraser. His answer: it was partly retaliation for last year's prolonged strike at Asbestos, Que., in which certain clerics defied the Duplessis government and supported labor. "Leader in this pro-labor, anti-Duplessis swing was Msgr. Joseph Charbonneau, Archbishop of Montreal, [who] last winter was summarily dismissed. Ostensibly he retired 'for reasons of health.' . . . Against Lévesque [and his followers] are all men who want Quebec to stay exactly as it is, or . . . as it was 50 years ago; for him, the men who believe change is imminent and overdue."

Church leaders were not pleased

over the belligerent and partisan *Maclean's* article. In Ottawa, Apostolic Delegate Msgr. Ildebrando Antoniutti said Fraser was "badly informed," his article "evidently tendentious." Archbishop Paul Emile Léger, who had been trying to pour oil over the controversial waters after the resignation of Msgr. Charbonneau, was rumored to be "unhappy."

This week the *Ensign,* Canada's national Catholic weekly newspaper, took a strong view of the Fraser article:

"This type of writing can most charitably be explained by reference to the hot weather. It appears as a great discovery for some non-Catholics when they hear of the existence of varying opinions amongst Catholics on many problems outside of faith and morals. Blinded by ignorance, sometimes innocent, they believe that all Catholics neither think nor discuss, but that they merely obey a dictatorial and usually arbitrary 'party line.' When they hear of discussions they see in it almost a rebellion, and then give their imagination free reign of misinterpretation . . ."

Debates of the Senate of Canada, 1944-45, June 21, 1944, pp. 210-218. (Speech of the Hon. Telesphore D. Bouchard).

The Gospel According to T. D. Bouchard

Honourable senators, one of the gaps that have been mentioned in the present debate as existing in the various history manuals used in English-speaking provinces of Canada is the omission of the statement that the French language is official in both Houses of our federal Parliament.

In my remarks on the resolution of the honourable senator from Sorel, I do not intend to criticize at length manuals in use in English- speaking provinces. . . .

I believe that on a question as delicate as the one under discussion it is better to leave to the citizens of each province the task of finding out and correcting for themselves the weaknesses in their own teaching of Canada's history. . . .

In the course of my remarks, I shall . . . point out some of the consequences resulting from a false interpretation of the history of Canada as it was taught and is still taught in the schools of my province. . . .

In speaking this language [English] I shall be compelled, much to my regret, to follow the advice of Monseigneur Laflèche, who once said—I was young then—"Speak English, but speak it badly". Our educators necessarily translated these words into "Teach English, but teach it badly". . . .

This motion has as its main purpose the placing in the hands of our children of any language and creed a text-book in which the main facts of our Canadian history shall be related according to truth, with due perspective, and interpreted in a way that will tend to create a real Canadian mind in all sections of this vast and promising country. . . .

Like my colleague from Sorel (Hon. Mr. David), I believe the time has long since come to improve the teaching of Canadian history in the schools of the province of Quebec. We have to judge a tree by its fruits, and I am sorry to state that the results we are actually reaping are far from being satisfactory. . . .

. . . Canadian history should not serve as a tool of subversive propaganda in the hands of those who are aiming to disrupt Confederation and overthrow our form of democratic government. . . .

I will show that Canadian history is badly taught in our schools, first by reading some excerpts from the lessons sought to be impressed on the receptive minds of our younger generation, and, secondly, by describing the subversive tendencies we actually find in a surprisingly large number of our educated men up to the age of forty—tendencies created by the way in which Canadian history is taught in our public schools. . . .

. . . I was fortunate in having as my first boss a Canadian of Scotch origin, although you would not have recognized him as such by the perfect French he spoke. In his office I learned that Canadians of English descent were not all cloven-footed and did not all bear horns, but on the contrary entertained the very same good sentiments as did we of French descent.

Why had I been led to believe those sillinesses? Why, like my young comrades, was I full of prejudices against those who were not speaking my language and not going to the same church? Since my infancy I had been taught that everything the French-Canadian had to suffer came from the fact that he was of French and Catholic descent. . . .

As I want to give my hearers the opportunity of verifying the accuracy of my quotations, I shall refer them to the text-book entitled: "History of Canada, Elementary Course, by the Brothers of Christian Science, approved by the Council of Public Instruction for primary schools, elementary grade, on the 11th of May, 1910—3rd edition". On page 72 I read:

> Paragraph 134—The English without taking into consideration the act of capitulation, abolished (1763) the French laws to replace them by those of England; all the Canadians were compelled under penalty of banishment to swear the Oath of the Test, or of supremacy, the heretical formula of which was revolting to the conscience of Catholics.
>
> Paragraph 135—General Murray, named Governor General (1763), mitigated the rigour of the new regulations and did not exact the Test Oath.

We have to note that these two conflicting paragraphs are on the same page, (72) and follow one another.

On the next page, (73), we read under the title "Canadian Clergy", paragraph 2:

> The clergy gave direction to the courage and the good-will of the still inexperienced Canadians; it helped them to withstand oppression and injustice and inspired a loyalty which forced England to give back to French Canada all the privileges conceded by the treaty of Paris.

May I point out that this treaty of Paris, which the author cites as a document by which England had conceded most important privileges to Canadians, is the very same treaty of which, on the opposite page it is said:

> —all the Canadians were compelled under penalty of banishment to swear the Oath of the Test, or of supremacy, the heretical formula of which was revolting to the conscience of Catholics.

How is it that the author can find some good in a treaty in which, according to the page following, he has seen only bad things for the Canadians? . . .

Now before closing this Canadian History, let us proceed to page 79 headed, "Narration—Anglicization." There we see the general appreciation of the author on the first decades of the English regime and the trend of the whole book. Here is the first paragraph in all its crudity:

> The end pursued by the policy of England in the early times of its administration in Canada was to anglicize the French-Canadian nation, to rob it of its religion, of its language and of its national customs.

It is true that at the end of the narration, after seventeen lines of the type of those I have quoted, the pupil can read:

> England ended by granting to the French-Canadians all the privileges possessed by free and independent peoples. . . .

The first point I wanted to make in

my remarks was that our history was not written as it should be for those who believe that harmony between the two great races living in this country is possible and most desirable. I have given a typical example of our Canadian history as it is taught in our Quebec schools. The contradictory statements I have quoted clearly demonstrate that this teaching cannot be according to facts, but is intended to prejudice young minds against our compatriots of a different tongue and creed. It is un-Canadian, even unchristian. The founder of Christianity has never preached that one man should rise against another because of differences of race and language.

The second demonstration I wanted to make was that those who taught Canadian history to divide the Canadian nation on racial and religious lines had now attained their ends to such an extent as to imperil our internal peace. . . .

History has taught us that nearly every revolution has started under the influence of secret societies. So, though there had been much preaching against secret societies, around 1928 one was founded with the blessing of the Catholic and French clergy. It bore the name of The Jacques Cartier Order and had its head office in Ottawa. Prominent French-Canadians were induced to join, the avowed practical end of the society being, not revolution, but to permit French-Canadians to have their fair share of the jobs in the public service. Later on, when the Jacques Cartier Order decided to expand beyond the capital, the strength of the order was to be applied to restraining what was called foreign investment in local trades, when these trades did not belong to French-Canadians. Anti-semitism also was called in to aid in the recruiting of members. Finally the officers of the highest degree gave, in the utmost secrecy, the watchword to invade the political field and to control patriotic societies, governments and public administrations of every kind.

. . . It is due to its secret organization that L'Union Nationale went to power in 1936, to give us the poorest and most abusive government in the history of our province . . .

Under the régime of L'Union Nationale, the first governmental offspring of the Jacques Cartier Order, regulations were passed in our province to shorten the English tuition in our schools, and a law was adopted to give precedence to the French text in our statutes, although the Constitution placed French and English on the same footing. No sane French-Canadian had ever asked for this change, as we were satisfied that the spirit of the law, as shown by one text or another, was the best guide for its interpretation. The enactment of our isolationists was the cause of such a commotion in the English section of the province that those who had caused the law to be inscribed in our statutes had to repeal it themselves. . . .

Some will blame me for having openly expressed my thoughts on Canadian History as taught in our Quebec schools, and especially for having shown what is going on in our upper and lower classes on the political situation behind the curtain, where the actors are rehearsing what many believe will be a farce, but which to my mind will eventually turn out to be a national tragedy. In a mounting storm I like to face the wind and not be caught by it in the back. I am not a pessimist, but when I hear distant rumblings of thunder I am aware that the dark clouds are liable to burst over my head.

Mémoires de T. D. Bouchard, vol. 3, (Montréal, Editions Beauchemin, 1960), pp. 176-178. (tr.)

Cardinal Villeneuve Rebuffs an Unnamed Man

"In the highest assembly of the country, a public figure, whom I need not name, recently made remarks about our province of Quebec which are as unjust and insulting as they were irrational and ill-founded. We cannot really explain such conduct in a man who extols honesty and equity, and whom I have always tried to understand and interpret with good will. I leave it to others to refute his charges of a political and racial nature. But, in no uncertain terms, I denounce his insinuations against the Church and the clergy. These remarks sound exactly the same and hide the same fanaticism as those of another sower of heresy whom most of our dissonant brothers disavow with humiliation. In the past, in the House of Commons, the Right Honourable Prime Minister of Canada has scarcely felt the need to hide his disdain for such supporters of national division, the only excuse for which is the grossest ignorance or congenital rabies. But, in the present case, what is all the more aggravating and particularly humiliating to the people of our province, and to all those across Canada who share the same blood, the same faith, and the same traditions of probity and Canadian fidelity, is that this unfortunate diatribe was delivered by one of our own. Public opinion will judge appropriately this challenge to our national consciousness.

As for myself, I will certainly make sure that the episcopate of this province does not unite with those movements that our insulter has so dishonestly confounded in order to vent his spleen better. But I must publicly condemn this flagrant insult to all that the French Canadian nation holds most dear: the authority and mission of its bishops, directly responsible for public instruction; and finally, the teachings of the Pope and of his noble representatives among us. For, it is only by an unintelligible, a not perfidious interpretation, of the speech which Mgr. the Secretary of the Apostolic Delegation delivered in this very city in 1937, at the fifteenth *Session de nos Semaines Sociales* that the orator who now arouses such general indignation, attempted to cast doubts upon the loyalty and the diplomacy of this prelate. . . .

. . . one is amazed at such a confusion of ideas, at such ignorance of the facts, . . . and at such a malicious style and text used under the pretence of independence and high politics. . . .

In the name of my venerable colleagues who are present here, in the name, I am sure, of the entire Catholic hierarchy of the country, I deny such unjustifiable denouncements and I openly declare that no one who follows the teachings of the Church and is faithful to the true French Canadian traditions is a threat to Canada, . . ."

Such was, in short, the speech of the Cardinal Archbishop of Quebec. A few days later and without any notice, I was fired from my job as president of Hydro-Quebec. The Prime Minister of the Province had to assume the role of executioner. . . .

Part V

Duplessis and the State: Vox Populi or Vox Duplessis?

From one point of view at least we can conclude that Duplessis and his party represented the voice of the people: his continued electoral successes are the proof. On the other hand, it is also evident that there was opposition to the *Chef,* his party and its policies. In an analysis of elections in the Province of Québec, Professor Jean Hamelin of the *Institut d'Histoire* of Laval University has shown that approximately 40% of the electorate voted Union Nationale, 40% Liberal and that the remaining 20% of the electorate swung their votes to one of the traditional parties or to a third party. To this voing pattern a comment must be added. There was little relationship between population distribution and representation. Duplessis inherited a system of electoral divisions which gave disproportionate representation to the rural areas. Montréal, for example, contained approximately 35% of the province's population; in the Legislative Assembly its deputies held about 15% of the seats. In 1956, Duplessis led the Union Nationale in an electoral campaign for the last time. His party received only 7½% more votes than did the Liberal Party. This moderate percentage difference resulted in the Union Nationale having a 32 vote majority in the Assembly.[1] However, in spite of the electoral system, Jean Lesage's Liberal Party won the 1960 provincial election. Was it the electoral system that was responsible? Or was it the personalities and policies of the opposing parties, and their support by the electorate?

In this section a few of the personalities and policies typical of Québec in the Duplessis era are presented. Through select issues such as fascism, the Padlock Law, communism, nationalism, education and the rôle of the élites we can examine the inter-

1. See Appendix: "Provincial Elections in Quebec, 1935-1956".

play of relationships which accounted for Duplessis' success and/or failures.

The Padlock Law is intimately linked with the name of Maurice Duplessis. To a lesser extent, his name is associated with fascism for, inasmuch as the Padlock Law was considered repressive and coercive, it was, therefore, fascist. This rather simple and naive interpretation is challenged by the anonymous article from *Saturday Night*. The author carefully distinguishes Québec's social reality from that reported in the newspapers of the day. The author also carefully indicates the original form of the Padlock Law and the acquiescence of Québecois and Canadian in moral and anti-communist crusades.

In the next selection Duplessis claims sole credit for the Padlock Law and in the *Montreal Star* article which follows we witness its threatened application . . . to truck drivers. Leslie Roberts, the author of the next reading, is a well-known Montréal journalist and broadcaster who has written extensively on Québec.

Can we conclude from these readings that Duplessis did or did not create the Padlock Law? Were his innovations radical ones? Further, was his use of the law out-of-step with the political, ideological and social realities of Québec, Canada and the world? That Duplessis was in tune with his times is a possibility. In 1951, according to a Gallup Poll, 83% of those Canadians interviewed believed that communists should be denied political office. Two years later, in 1953, only 26% of the Canadian sample believed that communists should have the right of free speech: 62% favored denying them this right.

Senator T. D. Bouchard's speech in the Senate of Canada has been presented in the section concerned with Duplessis, Québec and the Church. Sandwell and Frégault's views in this part express more generalized social reactions, English and French, in Québec and outside of Québec. The validity of Sandwell's interpretation, and its agreement with majority sentiment in Québec, then and now, should be subject to some questioning. Guy Frégault, the author of the second selection on Bouchard, is a well-known historian who has devoted his time since 1960 to the affairs of the *Gouvernement du Québec*. The Bouchard affair blended political and economic power, and social attitudes. Frégault's views express the *nationaliste* reaction to the Senator's history lesson. The firing of Bouchard from his post as president of Hydro-Québec was looked upon by some as nothing but economic revenge on the part of Duplessis, even though the Premier's policy was accepted by the majority of Quebeckers. This particular aspect of the issue masks another: does an important officer of a government body have the right to attack the government or the society it represents? Civil servants are usually supposed to be apolitical.

The use and/or abuse of Québec society and its idealogy, and of power, generally speaking, by Duplessis, his party and its governments led to what has been called a 'revolt of the intellectuals' in the early 1950's. Opposition to the Union Nationale was, of course, part and parcel of the Liberal Party's policy. However, until the election of Jean Lesage as party leader in 1958, opposition party leadership in the anti-Duplessis crusade was ineffective.

Vocal *anti-Duplessisme* centered about a new periodical, *Cité Libre*, founded in 1951, as well as in *Le Devoir*, once a vociferous supporter of Duplessis. The fountainhead of the revolt was Pierre Elliot Trudeau, a wealthy lawyer. Also in the group were Jean Marchand, a labour leader, Gérard Pelletier, a journalist, and a small handful of Québec literary luminaries. Collectively Trudeau, Marchand and Pelletier later became known as Québec's "three wise men."

This intellectual revolt is presented in broad terms in the article by Michael Oliver. At one time national president of the N.D.P., Professor Oliver is a political scientist who specializes in the affairs of French Canada. Two points are stressed in the selection: the desertion of the elite, and *anti-nationaliste* tendencies.

A specific difference between the Oliver piece and that of Fathers O'Neill and Dion which follows is that the former is by an English Canadian while the latter is by insiders. The two priest-authors held academic posts at l'Université Laval in Québec City This institution, as we have seen, was not popular with Duplessis or the Union Nationale government, although a later selection may modify this view somewhat. The approach of the clerics is typical of the blending of politics and morality in Québec society. The selection was written immediately after the 1956 election, an election in which Duplessis was once again returned to power.

Duplessis' dislike of Laval University was not, evidently, total. Gérard Pelletier's selection from a speech by the Rector of the university is typical enough of some of the rather fulsome praise bestowed on the Premier by many in the province. Education, however, was a provincial matter. On this subject even the rebellious intellectuals were agreed, as Pierre Elliot Trudeau informs us. The resolution of problems, in intellectual terms, is by means of political and constitutional equity. Legalism and not social change is the solution. This tendency to the interpretation of words is very characteristic of the supporters and adversaries of Duplessis: what people say is often more important than what people do.

From this consideration of Duplessis and the State of Québec, it is evident that monistic interpretations have little application. The State was not Duplessis nor was Duplessis the State. The differences of views among Anglophones within and without the province are fairly clear, as are the conflicting opinions amongst the Francophones in the province. Bouchard's speech, wildly applauded outside Québec, led to the loss of what little credibility the Senator had inside the province. Anti-communism was popular with all elements of the population. The revolt of the intellectuals did not defeat Duplessis: he died without that event ever taking place. The Union Nationale was defeated in 1960 by the Liberals; the Liberals were defeated by the Union Nationale in 1966. The explanation for the successes or failures of the Union Nationale and Duplessis remains to be discovered.

"Fascism in Canada. By a Non-Fascist," *Saturday Night*, vol. 53, no. 22, April 2, 1938, p. 2. Reprinted by permission of *Saturday Night*.

Preserve Liberty and Fight Fascism

As long as the allegations of the growth of fascism in Canada were confined to the columns of the "pink" Canadian journals I remained unmoved—since these valued organs are perpetually alarmed at the sad results of the obscurantist refusal in this country to follow Russia into a condition of pure liberty. When, however, the discussion reaches the columns of the London *Daily Herald,* I think that it is time for us to take it seriously.

That journal alleges that there are 80,000 organized fascists in the Province of Quebec alone—many of them drilling in armed bodies. I live in the Province of Quebec, and I have not seen these manifestations of the coming of dictatorship. Indeed, my own impression, for what it is worth, is that the correspondent of the *Daily Herald* must have been thinking of the annual parades of the snowshoe clubs the last few years. Every year Montreal is invaded by an enormous number of uniformed men and women, who march around the city clad in all their regalia. In recent years, by some sad mischance, they have succeeded in picking a day for the parade when there was no snow, and an Englishman, not understanding the finer points of Canadian humor, might have been misled into believing that these were not snowshoe clubs at all, but some mysterious organization established for a malign purpose. . . .

Be that as it may, however, I should like to stress the fact that the suggestion of handling the fight against communist propaganda in this way was not imported into this country from Italy or Germany, nor was it original in the Province of Quebec. The original Quebec padlock law was not the one recently passed by the Duplessis Government. It was passed by the Taschereau Government—which I never heard described as a fascist institution. It was copied from certain legislation in various States of the American Union. It was a law providing that premises used for prostitution, gambling, or such unpleasant customs, might be padlocked by the authorities.

The people who invented this idea were, as it happened, neither French-Canadians, Roman Catholics, nor fascists. They were highly advanced social reformers—chiefly members of Protestant communions, and not in the least interested in imposing the Mussolini-Hitler philosophy on us.

They were, indeed, precisely the same sort of people who, in Toronto, encourage the police authorities in certain measures of attack on social evils, which involve serious breaches of civil liberty. The plea behind this sort of thing is that there are certain forms of social evil so repugnant to the great majority of the people that they are essentially outlaw. There are men who would fight to the death to protect the ancient theory of the sanctity of a dwelling, and to insist that, in no circumstances, might a policeman or other agent of the state invade a residence except after obtaining a search warrant, as the result of sworn information that crime has been committed. These same men, in the case of one or two types of offences, feel that these constitutional protections of liberty might be set aside, and willingly back the state in entirely extra-legal, or very dubiously legal, measures to permit the police authorities greater freedom of action than they possess under the ordinary law.

It was on this model that the Government of the Province of Quebec undertook to pass the recent extension of the padlock law to cover premises where communism was taught.

The great majority of the people of the Province of Quebec happen to be members of the Roman Catholic Church, and that Church specifically lists communism as a sin. Communism is therefore highly repugnant to the majority of the people of the Province. It is a "social evil"—at least as serious, in their eyes, as any of those things which the worthy citizens of Toronto consider in this class. The authorities of the Province followed excellent precedents in attempting to combat it by ingenious measures of dubious legal value.

I cannot accept this case as evidence of fascism. In short, while I believe that, as I have tried to demonstrate above, there is plenty of fascism in Canada, I am forced to conclude that there is very little in the Province of Quebec. Most of the manifestations of fascism—if copying Italian and German methods of government be considered fascism—have occurred in Ontario and the Western Provinces.

I commend these ideas to those who, with me, wish to preserve liberty and to fight fascism.

"Duplessis Policy Is To Smash Reds", *Montreal Gazette,* Jan. 29, 1949.

The Padlock Law: Safeguard of Liberty

Quebec, Jan. 28.—Raiding of the premises at 5321 Park Avenue, Montreal, by the anti-Communist squad of the Provincial Police is in line with the determined policy of the government, declared Premier Duplessis today in the course of a press conference.

Incidentally, the premier said that information from a source well worthy of belief is that the man who signed the lease for the premises raid is City of Montreal councillor Max Bailey.

"The government of the province considers, and has always considered, that there cannot be any compromise with Communists or Communist propagandists, and in the speech from the throne this year we have declared that Communist propaganda is subversive, and has no place in the province of Quebec," said the Premier. "Communism is atheism, and our province is quite rightly attached to its religious and national traditions."

He again referred to the fact that it is an extraordinary thing that Canada should have representatives to Stalin countries, even after their odious treatment of the heads of the Roman Catholic Church in Hungary, and yet have no representative at the Vatican. Canada was linked through its representatives with the countries of persecutors and not with the representative of the persecuted.

As to the padlock law, Mr. Duplessis pointed out that this had been one of the first laws of his first government, the same principle being adopted against this moral contagion as is adopted against tuberculosis of the body. Even the adversaries of the legislation as carried out had given no cause for abuse, and it was to be noted that there were judgments of the courts to sustain the law.

The premier was pleased that Tim Buck, chief of an ideology which preaches atheism, disloyalty, disorder and sabotage, had declared that the padlock law in Quebec was paralysing Communist propaganda. There had been information that this ideology was making its headquarters at 5321 Park Avenue, and he had personally taken the necessary action to put the law into effect. This had followed representations from high authorities in Montreal asking that action be taken in regard to this locale.

It had been a duty to take the action which he had taken, added the premier. A great quantity of literature of a Communistic and atheistic nature had been seized.

Mr. Duplessis pointed out that despite what was said in some quarters, action taken under the padlock law was under jurisdiction of the courts, and subject to their approval.

"This law is a safeguard of liberty because it attacks in an effective manner, under the care of our courts, the worst enemies of liberty and democracy."

"Latest Red Ruse Exposed by Duplessis", *Montreal Star,* September 16, 1950.

No Truck with the Reds

Premier Duplessis yesterday reminded Québec truckers that their licences are issued for "recommendable purposes" and warned them not to carry communist propaganda in their trucks.

Some truckers, the Premier said, are using their trucks to distribute communist literature in the province and it was the government's intention to stop that. "We have been given information that communist propagandists, some operating in disguise, had used trucks circulating in the province to diffuse literature and propaganda that is atheistic, anti-patriotic, unwholesome and unfortunate." . . .

It was unfortunate, the Premier said, that the Canadian Postmaster General "gives so many facilities to communist propaganda." This referred to communist use of the mail, a subject about which Premier Duplessis has often spoken. "All deplore the activities and propaganda of the communists but not all take steps to prevent them." The province of Québec was "the only one to take steps to stop this perfidious propaganda."

He reminded truckers that the government had control over licencing of highway vehicles and that permits are issued for "recommendable purposes and not for illicit transport."

"I give this warning so none will protest innocence afterwards. We have the means at our disposal and we will use them. It may be recalled that permits used for travel on Quebec roads are given for recommendable ends and not for illicit transport."

Leslie Roberts, "Padlocks and Democrats", *Saturday Night,* vol. 54, no. 14, February 4, 1939, p. 3. Reprinted by permission of the Author.

Padlocks and Democrats

One point requires to be clarified in relation to discussion of Quebec's so-called Padlock Law; that is the attitude of the English-speaking and, generally speaking, Protestant minority resident in the province to the enactment and its enforcement.

In my travels beyond Quebec, particularly in Ontario, and through a reasonably comprehensive reading of the extra-mural press, the opinion has been gathered that the rest of Canada believes that the minority in the province of *soupe aux pois* is profoundly opposed to this law and the *gestapo* which its enforcement has set up. Nothing could be more remote from the truth. A majority of the English Canadians in Quebec either accept it as an excellent piece of legislation "which is keeping the Communists down," or tolerate it cheerfully because it has not affected them as individuals thus far. The viewpoint is one which needs to be set down, if only for the purpose of keeping the record straight. Permit me, also, to add that I am not a member of this majority within a minority. So far as I am concerned the Padlock Law is an abomination and I make no bones about saying so whenever opportunity offers. Most of my friends, I have noticed, look at me as if my only need is a donkey to ride, in order to become a first class tilter at windmills.

In order to understand this attitude it is necessary to comprehend the English Quebecker's mind, an instrument which does not operate in quite the same channel as does that of his Ontario brother. The English-speaking Quebecker, in the first place, is the most conservative-thinking of all Anglo-Canadians. He believes firmly in the rightness of things-as-they-are and has been weaned on a press which hammers home the idea every time the feeding-bottle appears on the news stands. Therefore he abhors the very word Communism with all the zeal with which Nature is alleged to abhor a vacuum; this without taking the trouble to look into the meaning of the term, or to examine the right of the individual to be a Communist if he wants to. If he has a religion, it sums up in the word Business, no matter whether Business involves attending an office from nine to five, selling goods or securities, or running a farm. Having done extremely well in the group sense by securing pretty much of a stranglehold on the Business of the province, while his colleagues of the other race have been playing with its politics, he leans to the view that he'll stick to Business and let Jean Baptiste make the laws and have the fun and excitement of enforcing them. So long as the Padlock Law is not invoked against himself the individual, therefore, he remains content to let it ride. To people like myself, who cannot abide the idea of surrendering so much as a jot of our hard-won liberty, he remarks that you might as well let the other fellows run the show, so long as they don't interfere with Business, and adds that obviously a service is being done all good citizens by "keeping the Communists down." Only today a banker said to me: "We're too law-abiding to care." In fine, he isn't interested. The fulminations of Mr. Calder and the Civil Liberties League, and all suchlike manifestations, he regards purely and simply as antics, as attempts to crash the limelight, and he will usually add that anybody with a grain of sense can see that all these defenders of the faith come pretty close to being Communists themselves. What can you do with that sort of fellow?

Yet he is a first-class citizen and, in his heart, a democrat. He believes profoundly in freedom, but it is his own personal freedom upon which he reflects, and like most democrats he manifests no interest in fighting for freedom and will not until his own individual liberty is threatened. Why should a man fight for an abstruse theory when he can get out and fight for more Business? That is the summation of the matter. He is proud that he is no politician, and this, he points out, is entirely a political matter. Let the politicians settle it.

If you have ever looked at the record, you may have noted that when the Padlock Law came before the provincial Legislature it was passed without a dissenting vote. In other words the Opposition approved it, and so did the handful of English-speaking members on the Government side. Some time later, when provincial Liberals assembled at Quebec to confirm Mr. Godbout as their leader, rumours were heard of an attempt on the part of English-speaking delegates to send down to the main convention a resolution calling for rescinding of the Act as a plank in the Opposition's platform. Nothing came of it. Instead the convention affirmed its liking for various sorts of freedom in one of those charmingly phrased and roundabout statements beloved of all Resolution Committees. If the truth of the matter were known a considerable number of English-speaking residents of Quebec who dabble in public affairs wouldn't attempt to touch the Padlock Law with the proverbial ten-foot pole, for the excellent reason that they have estimated it as charged with political dynamite and likely to explode into the teeth of anyone who attempts to knock it over.

Abrogation of the Padlock Law, therefore, will not be attempted by the English-Quebecker, certainly not by the minority acting in unison. Its defeat will come from within the ranks of the race whose political leaders instituted the law, and the first stirrings of organized attack upon it are beginning to be seen. Thus far one French-Canadian candidate for the Legislature—Raoul Trepanier in the recent Saint Louis by-election—has made rescindment a principal plank of his platform. In the recent municipal elections in Montreal several French-speaking candidates for aldermanic seats, two or three of whom were successful at the polls, came out openly against it. There are signs of open rebellion amongst various lay groups, not all of them communistic by any means, in the cities. In this direction lies settlement of the issue. Meanwhile those residents of other parts of the Dominion who have envisaged an English-speaking minority as up in arms against padlocks and other infringements of the liberty of the subject should change their estimate of the matter. The English element in Quebec, by which is meant the average English-speaking elector, excepting a highly vocal minority, simply doesn't care a snap of its fingers one way or another. But, then, *laissez faire* has always been our motto—and anyway, there's always Business to be chased, caught and pinned down in a corner. What's freedom by comparison?

B. K. Sandwell, "Bouchard's Speech May Be First Gun in Quebec Anti-Clerical War," *Saturday Night,* vol. 59, no. 44, July 8, 1944, p. 17. Reprinted by permission of *Saturday Night.*

The First Cannon Shot

The Toronto *Telegram* performed a public service on June 30 when it printed the entire text, a full newspaper page, of Senator Bouchard's speech, which is pretty certain to rank among the historic utterances of the Canadian Parliament—the more certain because the elements which resented it were so ill-advised as to demand his dismissal from his Quebec Hydro position, and so powerful as to be able to compel it.

It is possible, at that, that these elements acted under the pressure of somewhat urgent necessity. The elements which share the view quoted by Mr. Bouchard from a speech of the Chargé d'Affaires of the Apostolic Delegation in Canada—the view that French-Canadian Catholics must work for "a state completely Catholic, because such a country only can represent the ideal of human progress, and because a Catholic people has the right and the duty to organize itself socially and politically according to the tenets of its faith,"—these elements have been making fairly rapid progress in Quebec for about a generation, but there are indications that they are about to meet with somewhat more substantial resistance within French Canada itself. It is not of course by any means a tenet of the Catholic faith that a Catholic majority in a limited portion of the territory of a nation which is by majority non-Catholic must "organize itself socially and politically" as "a state completely Catholic," for that obviously involves secession from the larger non-Catholic nation. And there is a large and growing element among the French-Canadians of Quebec, an element which will be greatly reinforced when the service men and service women return, which is beginning to realize that the socio-political doctrines of Mgr. Mozzoni and of a part of the French-Canadian clergy can lead nowhere except to secession, and which does not desire to see those doctrines triumph.

HAS LACKED LEADERS

This element, I have said, is large and growing, and is obviously likely to be strengthened by anything which breaks down French-Canadian isolation. But it has lacked courageous and outspoken leaders, and these leaders cannot be found among the active politicians because it is too easy for such leadership to be represented to the less informed voters as constituting treason to the race and even to the Church. But Mr. Bouchard, retiring from active politics in the prime of life, with a long record of electoral victories and of useful public service, and an equally long record of devotion to the national unity of Canada, was obviously the ideal man to provide the leadership, to constitute the rallying point, and to raise the standard of complete inter-racial tolerance and harmony. If Mr. Bouchard could be, so to speak, knocked on the head at the first sign of the assumption of such leadership, it might well be hoped that it would be a long time before anybody else would dare to make a similar attempt. Dismissal from a public position involving a great deal of power and a salary of $18,000 a year may have seemed like a very good idea to Mr. Duplessis and the other politicians and journalists who demanded it.

But I am not quite sure that they counted the full cost, or realized the very limited scope of their victory. Mr. Bouchard is out of the Hydro. But he is not out of journalism, and he is not out of the Senate (nobody seems to have thought of impeaching him) and he is not in my opinion in the least likely to be terrorized or silenced. And he has been made to appear as a martyr for the cause of liberal thought and broad Canadianism, and his speech has been given an enduring importance which it might have lacked. No action could have more emphatically suggested to impartial-minded persons that it was a speech to which no other effective reply could be made.

The question of the exact size and influence of the Order of Jacques Cartier is of minimum importance. Several eminent French-Canadians have declared that they know nothing of it, and have apparently supposed that it therefore cannot exist. But Mr. Bouchard named its open or popular newspaper organ, which certainly does exist for I have seen plenty of copies of it, and it teaches the precise doctrines which he described; and he quoted at length from its secret organ, and the quotation has not been denied. But the name, the size, the secrecy of the inspiring organization are a minor matter. The major matter is the doctrines and the direction in which they lead. They are the doctrines of the corporative state *à la* Portugal and the corporative state *à la* Portugal is not possible in a Quebec which continues to form a part of the Dominion of Canada.

Saturday Night suggested last week that this was a private fight among French-Canadians. To a large extent I still believe that to be true. If Quebec after mature consideration should decide that it desires to secede from the Dominion I cannot quite imagine the other provinces seeking to retain it by force. But we have a right to be interested in the decision and the process by which it is arrived at; and those of us who desire the unity of all Canadians and are willing to make all possible concessions to the legitimate views and interests of French Quebec have a right to wish well to those who in that province are seeking to keep alive the corresponding desire for Canadian unity.

Guy Frégault, "La prédication de M. Bouchard," *L'Action Nationale,* vol. 29, no. 3, March 1947, pp. 165-168. (tr.) Reprinted by permission of *L'Action Nationale.*

Bouchard Discovers America

. . . There is scarcely a question which Mr. T.-D. Bouchard does not cover . . . . [I]n thick waves of his inspired eloquence . . . last January . . . he proposed a new system of education aimed at strengthening what he calls Canadian unity. . . .

This unity . . . is not unattainable, continues Mr. Bouchard. To achieve it, "we must find a new method for our system of public education. We should have a national school system." Here, be patient, another definition is required: "By national schools, I mean schools which would be acceptable to all Canadians: Catholics, Protestants, non-Christians and all those people of all religions who believe in the superiority of non-confessional schools." . . .

The preceding quotations are drawn from a report in *La Presse.* (30 January, 1947). That of the *Gazette* . . . is more complete. In it appears the following sentence: "This panel would solve the problem of many Canadians of French descent who are seeking schools for their children with no risk of seeing them transformed from broad-minded youths to narrow-minded nationalistic adults." Might the senator be insinuating that Catholic instruction maintains a "narrow spirit" of "nationalism" among us? He would thus be tacitly admitting that neutral instruction is not only a danger to our faith but also to our patriotism.

It is as clear as day that such instruction threatens our faith. All Catholics know this. In this regard, the Rev. Father Gaudrault is justified in recalling Christian doctrine, the traditional doctrine of the Church such as Pius XI once expressed it: "In fact, inasmuch as education consists essentially of moulding man, of teaching him what he should be and how he should behave in this earthly world in order to attain the sublime end for which he has been created, it is clear that there can be no true education that is not entirely directed towards this final end. Furthermore, in the present order of Providence, that is, since God revealed himself through his only Son, who is the only 'Way, Truth and Life', there cannot be a complete and perfect education except for a Christian education." One will understand that, personally, I prefer this doctrine—if I dare make an odious comparison—to that old-fashioned, threadbare ideology outlined by Mr. Bouchard's foolish definitions.

It is also obvious that neutral education would endanger our patriotism . . . our minorities know something about this question. Having studied the history of French instruction in minority schools in Canada with as much science as sympathy, Canon Groulx concluded: "Without doubt, it is undeniable that the educational controversies have everywhere taken on the character of national quarrels or ethnic conflicts. Can we blame anyone other than these persecutors who, in their totalitarian fanaticism, never separate the French school from the Catholic school?"

To those in the front ranks who have fought and are still fighting to save our spiritual wealth, the country of Quebec must speak with a voice other than that of resignation. Its words must be sensible, courageous and dignified. This is why we have challenged Mr. Bouchard's proposals. He who says nothing consents . . . it would be too easy to confuse a contemptuous silence with a consenting silence . . . we do not consent.

As for the actual preaching . . . it's old hat . . . the senator thinks he is discovering America. Someone should have the charity to tell him that it has already been done.

Michael Oliver, "Duplessis and Quebec's Intellectuals, *Canadian Forum,* vol. XXXVIII, no. 449, June 1958, pp. 55-57. Reprinted by permission of the Author.

Pre-republican China and Duplessis

In Chinese history, one of the signs that a dynasty's fortunes were on the wane was the desertion of the intellectuals. The political distance between pre-republican China and *Union Nationale* Quebec would require some tricky measurement, but French Canada's traditional respect for things immaterial may make the intellectual's attitude to the political regime worth study. Donations from corporations owned by English Canadians and Americans provide the solid bone structure of Quebec's dominant party, and to this adheres a bulk of well-fattened members. . . .

The elite's "desertion" from the Union Nationale is, however, a striking fact of the present period and this movement away from the party and what it represents must, in part, be explained in terms of profound changes in Quebec society. Intellectuals had to find a place to go if they were to leave the world dominated by a party which claimed to embody the main political tradition of French Canada—nationalism and provincial autonomy. Only since the war have institutions outside the traditional framework grown up enough to provide careers to those who did not conform in their social and political thinking. Most of the escape routes of the past involved a violent de-nationalisation operation which only the most hardy could survive in comfort, and which few relished even if they were capable of withstanding it. Fitting into attractive posts in business or in the federal civil service demanded a quasi-anglicization at least, a severing of ties with the society of family, parish and school. Those that did make the break lost their influence in the sphere from which they had come. They were thus not a new element in French Canadian society, they were outside it. . . .

Within these purely French Canadian institutions it has been possible to explore far beyond the social and political boundaries of traditional French Canada. The penalties for unorthodox ideas and behaviour are applied at a much further point of deviation than was (and is) the case in older organizations. When, in 1944, Senator T. D. Bouchard . . . launched his famous attack on the nationalist *Ordre Jacques Cartier* and the French Canadian nationalist bias in Québec schools, he was dismissed from his post as head of Hydro-Québec, and never regained his former stature. Yet Pierre Trudeau's attack on the nationalist tradition in a recent book has intefered not at all with his career as a labour lawyer, as a perennial CBC panelist and commentator and, generally as an active force in his province. . . .

There have been attempts to break away from traditional orthodoxy before, but they have usually borne fruit only in two ways. The first is a rebellious criticism which, because it never gets a chance to act, because it is never faced with the challenge of putting ideas into practice, spends its energies in lone assaults on the existing framework. The careers of critical journalists like Olivar Asselin or Jules Fournier were of this type. So, in a way, was the career of Henri Bourassa, as both politician and journalist. The second is the way of aestheticism. The protest of certain groups in French Canada in the thirties, because they could not be channelled into existing institutions, took the form of individual creative activity in art, in poetry and in literature. Let there be no mistake about it, these roles are of vital and lasting importance. The rebel and the independent artist are in no way inferior to those who act through collective institutions. But their roles are different—different from that of trade union leader who faces the tasks of organizing, calling strikes, collective bargaining; different from that of the men responsible for developing a new medium of mass communication. The latter functions are performed through institutions which give opportunities to a much larger number to develop an independent, non-traditional point of view, for it is not everyone who has the capacity for rebellion, or individual artistic creativity, in an unreceptive environment. Furthermore, those who centre their activities about both these modern careers are conscious of accomplishment in a French Canadian context which is directly comparable to similar achievements in the rest of North America. They are not "surviving" as French Canadians, they are living and creating something which stands up under any criteria of comparison. Relations with English Canada tend, for this reason, to be easy and confident, and the "protectionism" of the Union Nationale much less attractive.

For the majority of Quebec's intellectuals, however, the traditional institutional framework provides still the most readily available careers. In many such positions, opportunities for critical analysis and for promoting social and political change do exist. A career in journalism always gave some scope to independence. But it could only consistently do so if the journalist was attached to an independent and adventurous newspaper. *Le Devoir* has usually played this role in French Canada, except perhaps for a period from the late twenties to the end of the war, when its nationalism became merely a right-wing traditionalism. Certainly today it must be ranked among the major forums of dissent from the Duplessis regime and from the narrow formulas of an anachronistic ideology. But its opposition is protest within a nationalistic autonomist framework, and in this it differs from the newer institutions open to Quebec's intellectuals.

The universities of Quebec are in a somewhat similar position to a newspaper like *Le Devoir,* in that they are institutions of an older society which are only gradually transforming themselves to meet the challenge of a new era. . . . But the bounds of this independence have at times been very narrow indeed, for the universities and colleges have always been reliant on church and state. Among the newer, non-traditional disciplines—the physical and social sciences—the process of developing new ways of dealing with Québec's problems has advanced most rapidly. It is no coincidence that the first president of the *Rassemblement* (an organization for education in democracy and reform) came from the Science Faculty of the University of Montreal and the second from the Social Sciences Faculty at Laval.

The desertion of the intellectuals is thus under way. But it is by no means complete. And the deserters lack political form. The provincial Liberal party is in poor shape indeed and it will take more than the coming provincial convention to convince many of Quebec's intellectuals that it is capable of creating a new political atmosphere in the province. The Parti Social Démocratique (Québec's CCF) has not yet overcome longstanding difficulties in attracting French Catholic support. The current move of Jean Drapeau, Montreal's ex-mayor, beyond the confines of municipal politics bears watching. But Drapeau's chief force thus far seems to come from clerical sources opposed to vice and political immorality, and disgruntled small businessmen.

Intellectuals who remain with Duplessis may be a dwindling force, but they are by no means negligible. Among them are, first, the truly conservative nationalists. They are a group whose ideas have not evolved appreciably since the days of Bishop Bourget; a group which sees a communist behind every bush (and especially those planted by English Canadians) and which will neither forgive England and English Canada for the Conquest, nor France for the Revolution. Men like Robert Rumilly and Léopold Richer desire the closed society in its most rigorous sense.

Another group of at least quasi-intellectual supporters of Duplessis come from the traditional professions—law and medicine. Substantial careers can be made in both these fields without any appreciable contact with the rest of Canada. Their clientele is often exclusively French-Canadian, and no changes in Quebec's social and political structures offer them particular advantages. Their conservatism is based on self-satisfaction and inertia, although patronage considerations as well affect some of the lawyers. . . .

A third category includes certain secondary school teachers—especially those in orders—and some university professors. Academic willingness to accommodate M. Duplessis is partly based on a realization that Quebec's educational system is badly in need of overhauling, and that drastic change can involve acute discomfort for those who direct its schools. . . . In addition, educators are painfully conscious of their reliance on the good will of the provincial government for a major part of their funds, and they know that institutions which question the policies of the government expose themselves dangerously. The tensions between those who share these fears and those who are anxious for immediate and thoroughgoing change were brought to light dramatically at the provincial conference on education which took place early in February. On one hand, this conference by a vote of 70 to 64 supported the principle of free tuition for all levels of education—a radical proposal indeed. On the other hand, it amended a resolution on the question of state aid to education in such a way as to ensure that "la Conférence n'ait pas l'air de blâmer le gouvernement provincial."

In a more general sense, those intellectuals who continue to support the Union Nationale share two common features: lack of confidence in French Canada's ability to survive close contact with the rest of North America and a strong attachment to those things which are distinctively French Canadian. . . . Lack of confidence in French Canada does not necessarily lead to enthusiasm for Duplessis' provincial autonomy position. It can just as well result in a desire to merge with English-speaking North America, a desire to give up the struggle for *survivance* altogether. Again, attachment to those things which make French Canada unique is not enough. The best proof of this is the nationalism of *Le Devoir.* Its editors have again and again pointed out that Duplessis regards provincial autonomy as a possession to be defended rather than a positive duty which must be fulfilled. Many nationalists who realize that they must create a modern, progressive provincial administration if they are effectively to compete (or co-operate!) with Ottawa lost patience with the Duplessis regime's incompetent conservatism long ago.

French Canadian intellectuals who lack confidence in the ability of their society and its institutions to withstand abrupt change in close contact with English Canadian organizations are not necessarily the victims of misplaced and illusory timidity, nor does their lack of confidence imply a sense of the inferiority of Quebec's institutions. The problem of sheer weight of numbers in any intimate relationship with English Canada cannot be shrugged off. The feeling that institutions of a minority have to be firmly rooted before they can safely ally themselves, or merge, with those of the majority is not irrational, although it may often be exaggerated disproportionately. . . . A steadily increasing number of intellectuals believe that M. Duplessis' neglect of the province's social, economic and educational needs is sufficient reason for opposing him. . . .

Perhaps those English Canadians who deplore the difficulties M. Duplessis creates for all of Canada can act most constructively by making sure that in joint English Canadian-French Canadian undertakings—conferences, national associations, etc.—the French Canadian position receives its due weight. . . . Precautions such as these can never wholly overcome the reluctance of some nationalist intellectuals to enter into associations which presuppose an English Canadian majority. But they may help to ensure that the defence of provincial and cultural autonomy does not always take the form of Quebec's Union Nationale regime.

Gérard Dion et Louis O'Neill, "L'immoralité politique dans la province de Québec," *Le Chrétien et les Elections,* (Montréal, Editions de l'Homme, 1960), pp. 113-123. (tr.) Reprinted by permission of Les Editions de L'Homme.

A Sorbid Boon

The province of Québec has just chosen [1956] the men who will hold public office for the next four years. . . .

. . . in view of certain methods used in the recent election campaign, and the consequences that might ensue, we consider it a very serious duty to pause for at least a few moments to analyse the situation.

The wave of stupidity and immorality which Québec has just witnessed cannot leave any lucid Catholic indifferent. Perhaps, never before has the religious crisis which exists here been more clearly manifested. Never before have we been furnished a more striking proof of the dechristianization taking place among the masses.

. . . Those who consider morality to be merely a problem of shorts, sun dresses or the Padlock Law will find the remarks made here quite daring. However, Christian morality . . . which sets up charity, truth and justice as the fundamentals of social life, and which is still shocked at lies, perversion of consciences and systematic corruption of the law cannot help but be moved by the state of affairs now all too evident. . . .

A Christian community in which lies become systematic is a community in which religious beliefs are inevitably attacked, for the Christian faith is first of all a cult of the truth. The modern methods of diffusing ideas enable people to construct immense collective lies, and to repeat denunciatory slogans through the press, radio and television to the saturation point, to such an extent that the man in the street can no longer resist and is so willing to accept, that "they become true." This technique, perfected by Hitler, was adopted by the communists. It is now part of our electoral customs. Lies are used to cultivate the complexes and fears of the masses, to distort opponents' ideas, and to destroy personal reputations. If they are well phrased they can make Christians accept clearly non-Christian attitudes. For example, they might contend that to advocate social security is to silde towards Marxism, to champion health insurance is to undermine our religious communities, to feed hungry people in underdeveloped countries is to impoverish us and to encourage communism, etc. . . .

The use of myth is an integral part of the vast campaign to spread slogans. Myth is the apparent or idealized value proposed in place of the true value. . . . It is less often pure fiction than the systematic corruption of a badly known reality. Western capitalism, as presented to the people of the Soviet Union, is partially a myth. The Jewish problem was a favorite myth of Hitler. . . . The cult of myths is immoral because it destroys truth, the finest flower of the soul. It degrades the intellect, enslaves man, channels the blind energies of the masses and makes them dangerously easy for agitators and demagogues to control. . . .

Communism, as presented to the masses in Quebec, is a myth. . . . The theme of anti-communism has been used in almost identical terms by well-known clerics, recognized fascists, despicable third-rate politicians and out and out hoodlums. . . .

Systematic lies and the use of myth are fraudulent manoeuvres. Procedures such as buying votes, undermine the electoral laws, threatening reprisals against those who do not support the "right party," false oaths, impersonation, and bribing electoral officers, also seem to be becoming normal elements of our social life during election periods. Some urban districts have seen examples of the use of violence that would make the most fervent anarchists jealous. . . .

Here as well, what should worry us even more is that so few people appear shocked by all this. Similar methods used in a communist country make our brave people indignant and set our zealous Catholic journalists into action. In Quebec, these methods are rapidly gaining open public acceptance. We even brag and laugh about them as if they were part of an innocent game. . . .

This, unfortunately, is a characteristic of the French Canadian people, which is becoming more and more evident. We have fallen a long way since that day when one of our great theologians declared that we were destined above all for noble ideas and apostolic missions! Several cases have been brought to our attention in which electors not only failed to resist an offer to sell his vote but openly offered it in exchange for money or generous gifts. In this way, they were paid for repairs to roofs, hospital bills, . . . etc.—and this does not take into account the procession of refrigerators and television sets received. . . .

What is most curious is that, in general, these people still say their prayers at home, keep a sharp eye on their children's morality, and denounce the fallacious conduct of the Jehovah's Witnesses. They hardly ever accuse themselves of being unjust. . . . We do not call this hypocrisy. It is simply a failure to realize the extent of the sickness. . . .

If we bear in mind the electoral mores of our province, each election appears to present an opportunity for killing the democratic spirit and for further installing a socialist spirit into our population. As surprising as this may seem, inasmuch as our political parties brandish the spectre of socialism and communism before the people as a bugbear which must be overcome, it nonetheless remains a most obvious truth, so obvious that none realizes it.

In fact, what is the socialist spirit? Socialism, as condemned by the church, in addition to its materialistic nature, is based on a false conception of the State and its relations with the individuals and the groups that make up civil society. The socialist spirit exists when the State is everyone's good angel, and when it interferes in all those groups making up civil society and tries to control them. The socialist spirit exists when the State is omnipresent and when nothing can be done without it. . . .

[The use of religion] is a tactic to which our electoral technicians have commonly resorted. The procedure has simply become more refined and ignoble. They have gone about it unscrupulously, everywhere denouncing the pseudo-enemies of religion and succeeding in activating the defense mechanisms of believers whose good will far surpasses their critical spirit.

Anti-communist slogans seem to have been used with considerable success. Popular literature has penetrated the presbyteries and convents. A vicar changed his convictions after reading Adrien Arcand's *Unité Nationale*! Nuns read or heard strange stories about people, who, until then, were believed to be Catholic. People spoke about the threat to the faith, the enemies prowling around, and about the lesson to be learned from the experience of those countries in which a mere handful of communists had succeeded in gaining power, etc. Seen from close up, it was shoddy merchandise. . . . And yet, the trick worked marvellously well. . . .

A few priests plunged headlong into the scuffle. In a parish in a Quebec suburb, a vicar stretched his paternal rôle to the point of not only speaking from the pulpit in favour of his candidate, but went so far as to solicit votes from door to door. Another case: a vicar in the same county advised people to vote for the candidate whose party was in power: "Otherwise, we get nothing." Another: "Vote for whomever you wish, but when we have a good government, we should keep it." A last case: "Before going to vote, don't forget to look at our fine new school." . . .

To conclude, we believe that we should admit our negligence as social critics. We have concentrated on certain labour relations problems, and have not sufficiently helped our colleagues to elaborate a political morality. . . . This task is not easy, for we will have to face many vested interests, entrenched ideas and prejudices. . . . St. John the Baptist and many other martyrs learned only too well that it is dangerous to preach political morality . . . we do not intend to shirk this duty.

Gérard Pelletier, "Les amitiés particulières", *Cité Libre,* vol. 2, nos. 1-2, June-July 1952, pp. 64-65. (tr.) Reprinted by permission of the Author.

Peculiar Friendships

The following paragraphs are extracts from a speech delivered by Mgr. Ferdinand Vandry, Rector of Laval University, at the inauguration of the School of Commerce. The Rector's speech was taped.

"Ladies and gentlemen, the Government of the Province [of Quebec] has done a great deal for this University. The forestry building stands as proof of this. This School for Advanced Commercial Studies will attest to it even more for generations to come; and other buildings which will be created, which will soon rise up over this campus, will also demonstrate it. We have benefited greatly from the largesse and generosity of the provincial government, and I wish to take advantage of this opportunity, rather it is my duty, one in which I take great pleasure, to thank the Honourable Maurice Duplessis for all that we owe him, for all that he has done for this University. And if anyone knows how much we owe the Honourable Maurice Duplessis, it is I. No one in this University is as close to the Prime Minister as the Rector of Laval, and I thank Divine Providence for this, and I also thank the courtesy and kindness of the Honourable Prime Minister for it.

"Well, I know intimately many things that you do not; I know of the generosity shown us both by the right and by the left, I know that certain sums of money have been contributed to the University's coffers over the past few years without this being made public, with the matter remaining unknown except to the Rector and his immediate Counsellors, and I know that we owe all this to the graciousness, the generosity and the great amiability, I was going to say and I will say, the sincere friendship that M. Duplessis has shown the Rector of Laval University, just as he knows that, in return, he can count on the sincerity and on the tenacity of the deep friendship of the Rector of Laval. I wanted to say this because I believe that the Honourable Maurice Duplessis, as well as his government, but specially he, deserves it; moreover, I know that you are happy to learn of what the government has done for us, what we should thank the Prime Minister for."

Undoubtedly Mgr. Vandry said "by the right and by the left" to avoid exciting jealousies, for we are deeply convinced that these "sums of money" came mainly from the right.

Furthermore, the Rector of Laval would be wise to specify, in his next speech, whether public or private funds were involved. In the first case, we would be less than pleased to learn that our taxes could take the road (even the correct road) to the coffers of Laval University "without this being made public, with the matter remaining unknown except to the Rector and his immediate Counsellors."

Pierre Elliott Trudeau, "Les octrois fédéraux aux universités," *Cité Libre*, no. 16, February 1957, pp. 9-13; 28-31. Reprinted by permission of the Author and The Macmillan Company of Canada Limited.

I Agree With... Some of Mr. Duplessis' Attitudes

There is something rotten in the State of Denmark. For on this question of [University] grants, I find myself at variance with most of my friends and with people whose thought generally pleases me. Furthermore, I entirely agree with certain attitudes of Mr. Duplessis and the nationalists, people with whom I do not usually side.

However, I will not make my position clear to either one side or the other unless I am permitted to make a few remarks before hand. . . .

In a Federal State such as Canada, the situation is . . . complex. The exercise of sovereignty is divided between a central government and ten regional governments which together make up the *Canadian State,* and which individually are responsible for a part of the commonweal. Now, as the same citizens vote in Federal and provincial elections, they must be able to determine easily which government is responsible for what: otherwise the democratic control of power becomes impossible.

Now, the constitution itself effects this devolution of responsibilities: provincial governments must tend to the commonweal of those people within their jurisdiction in all matters which come under (among others) article 92 of the British North America Act, and the central government has a similar responsibility under article 91. But, as a corollary, no government—for that part of the commonweal *for which it is not responsible*—has a right to oversee the administration of any other government. . . .

It inevitably follows from the above principles that the total wealth available to the Canadian treasury should be divided between the Federal and provincial governments so that each may fulfil its public responsibilities as it sees them. This principle might prove difficult to apply in a very poor country; for here, when taxable wealth cannot meet the needs of both the central and the local governments, the question of priorities arises; namely, should central responsibilities (e.g., foreign affairs) take priority over local ones (e.g., education). Fortunately, however, such a choice need not be made in Canada. . . .

"Is university education a provincial responsibility?" Léon Dion asked on concluding a very clever exposé. And he answered: "The university should not fall within any sphere of influence at all." *(Le Devoir,* Nov. 5, 1956).

Unless this reply is intended to lead us far from the accepted theories of legal sovereignty towards some form of pluralistic anarchy, I take it to resemble the position adopted by Maurice Blain: "Should not our universities, caught between two ineluctable masters . . . meet their economic needs by constantly playing off the Federal and provincial powers against each other?" *(Le Devoir,* Nov. 2, 1956).

I do not *a priori* declare that education (at least university education) should never fall within a concurrent Federal jurisdiction: it might be in the public interest for the central State to attempt immediately to extend the frontiers of our culture, or to take over the wholesale production of technicians so that we could deal with our underdevelopment, our competitors and our enemies. However, that would have to be proven. And in particular, as a citizen, I would insist that such a revolutionary interpretation of the constitution be made the object of a conscious choice. I would insist on the need for political parties to take clearly defined positions in this debate, to explain their arguments, and to go before the electorate so that the latter would have the opportunity to decide with a full knowledge of the issues involved. . . .

By offering grants to universities, the federal government could have made a constitutionally acceptable offer of mutual aid.

But it erred by linking this gesture to a fiscal system which was incompatible with a harmonious federalism. We still remember how, not so long ago, provincial autonomy was almost undermined by fiscal agreements of this kind. Surely, the Federalists have not yet sufficiently demonstated their solicitude for the provinces. . . . The provinces find it insulting to be offered as a gift what M. Saint-Laurent admits is their own taxpayers' money. And this undermines the principles of representative democracy. . . .

Thus, the Federal government must try to revise its fiscal practices so that the provinces and the municipalities can draw on a taxing power which is sufficiently large to meet their obligations.

So long as this is not done, we might legitimately suspect that Federal gifts are tainted with bad faith. And remember this at election time. . . .

[Universities] could have accepted the Federal grants, had M. Saint-Laurent first explained to them the principles that had inspired them.

Academics are also electors, and influential ones to boot. If they had understood the situation a little better, they could have both benefited from the grants and made the Federal government accept sounder theories of federal finances.

Then M. Duplessis would have been forced by his own autonomist logic to pass a law forbidding universities to accept Federal grants. The debate on such a law in the Legislature would have prevented the Liberal opposition from hedging as they did on November 20. In this way, the electorate would be one step closer to maturity, and the universities one step closer to a recognition of their responsibilities.

But it now seems to be commonly accepted that secret negotiation convinced all of Quebec's universities to refuse the grants. This refusal is not fatal *per se* for, by a clause, the astuteness of which I admire, those grants which are not accepted now, are not completely lost: they will accumulate until that day when they are so large that the Quebec electorate will feel the full weight of rapacious centralizing forces, which will be opposed by mere verbal autonomy.

On the other hand, all will be lost if university authorities hide behind a wall of secret diplomacy and of *combinazione,* as they have already begun to do. The people will become even more ignorant of educational needs. the universities will have new task masters, and politicians in Ottawa and Quebec will continue to play football with the constitution. . . .

We do not object to the provincial

government's autonomist policy; rather we object to the purely negative and basely partisan aspect of this policy. Let us hope that M. Duplessis tries to form an administration that will rival the efficiency and honesty of the Federal government; this would be genuine rivalry. Let him provide universities and the entire school system with the means to fulfill the rôle. Let him by provincial generosity in this area make Federal grants . . . appear insignificant. Let him propose constructive alternatives, rather than mere refusals. . . . Let him by his ability and good faith place the Federal government on the defensive in these areas. . . .

But these are New Year's wishes, and just as futile. For M. Duplessis believes that we have the cleverest people, the best system of education and the best government in the world. And the greatest provincial Prime Minister since Confederation.

Part VII

Ecce Homo

Public figures have their personal histories. Before Duplessis became a politician he had been moulded by his family, his language, his religion, his education, his profession and the specific social milieu in which he had grown up. He was also moulded by each issue he faced, resolved, or failed to resolve. His experience as an opposition member, premier, defeat in 1939 and electoral successes from 1944 till his death all contributed to shaping the man.

Till now Québec in the Duplessis era has been presented by themes. This last section is more personal: it concerns the man. Duplessis himself was a pragmatist; retrospection was not a notable characteristic of his personality. Judgement of the man and his times is left to others; eventually, judgment becomes the task of the historian and the student of history.

Each of the selections that follows represents a view of Duplessis. They reflect the personality and politics of the author as much as the personality and politics of Duplessis.

The *Saturday Night* article, written on the eve of Duplessis' last electoral campaign, accurately reflects the principal bias of the English press: the Duplessis era was Duplessis, no more, no less. The selection's unflattering reference to *Le Chef's* birth date reflects a generalized non-Québec view of the man.

The late editor of *Le Devoir,* André Laurendeau, was responsible for the Negro King interpretation of Duplessis. Again the premier's personality is stressed, but so are responses of the men and the society that worked hand in hand with *Le Chef.* Duplessis' responsibility, Laurendeau suggests, is equalled by the acquiescence of his tribe.

Pierre Laporte, at one time a journalist, and now a Liberal member of the National Assembly of Québec, was a political enemy of Duplessis, yet the author cannot avoid a very sympathetic representation of his foe. The emphasis on personality is there, but of a very different order than that usually found in the Canadian press.

The last reading, written by François-Albert Angers, an economist as well as the editor of *L'Action Nationale,* attempts an assessment of Québec in the Duplessis era. In 1960, Duplessis' party was defeated. The *révolution tranquille* began. In 1966 the party that Duplessis founded was returned to power.

How do we evaluate Duplessis? Some writers depict him as a constructive force in Quebec political life; others make unflattering parallels. There has been a tendency to say that his era died with him while others claim that his legacy is with us yet. On the one hand he is presented as a far-seeing statesman who boldly led his people, his society, his province into the 20th century; or again, he was an abomination, a selfish and corrupt politician interested mainly in personal power.

We began with one general question: was the Duplessis era in Québec representative of the will of the people? If yes, then it was a democratic society. Or, was the government of Québec in the years of Duplessis' mandates nothing more than the will of *Le Chef*? That would be dictatorship.

"Persona grata, The Old Chief", *Saturday Night,* vol. 71, no. 3, April 14, 1956, pp. 15-17. Reprinted by permission of *Saturday Night.*

The Same Day as Hitler

Quebec is getting ready for the provincial general elections in June. And the Chief himself, after a pre-Easter recuperation in the Bahamas—staying, appropriately enough, at the British Colonial Hotel—while preparing for his seventh campaign as leader of his party, and, no doubt, for his fifth term as Prime Minister of Quebec. The immediate question is: will he stand the strain? He is 66 years of age, an advanced diabetic with a chronic sensitivity about his physical condition, which is the subject of widely-differing assessments. But the prodigy who undertook his last campaign in a steel corset, from the effects of a serious spinal injury in the previous months, is still likely to brace himself for a good performance.

The election, it is being said, will be a domestic affair, a "quiet one", comparatively speaking. After the recent tax concessions by Ottawa and in the prevailing mood of peaceful co-existence, it is difficult to see how the more dramatic issues of the past can be revived, or the more colorful irrelevancies be effectively sponsored. There will be a chance, at least, to look at the record, at what the Premier has and has not done during 15 years of power. And there will, probably, be a wider inclination to look at the man himself—at Maurice LeNoblet Dupplessis—in perspective, as he nears the end of the road, dispassionately and, perhaps, a little compassionately.

There is something almost pathetic today about this man with the caricaturist's nose and the old-fashioned collars, who has been so full of life and wit, so much a part of the Quebec scene, sitting alone with grey, drawn features in his suite at the huge gloomy Hotel Frontenac, sipping orange juice, watching the World Series on TV as his one relaxation. The man who boasted that he had never opened a book since he left school is increasingly obsessed with a superstitious form of religion about which even some of the priests are cynical. There is a growing note of self-pity, of reproach for ingratitude; of vindictiveness, and, all the time, this obsession with the power to which so much has been sacrificed, which is yet so sterile and insubstantial. In an odd kind of way, Duplessis is coming to resemble the butt of his favorite jokes—"Mackenzie King Stink"—in his last years, though not, happily, in the matter of money.

The story of Duplessis is, itself, a fairly simple one. He comes from the small-town, *petit bourgeois*—not, as some reporters claim, from the Quebec elite. But his father, who married a girl of Scots-Irish descent, became a Judge in Three Rivers, and remained obstinately in opposition to the old Liberal regime.

Maurice was born on April 20, 1890 (the same day as Hitler), an only son, and seems to have led a fairly uncircumscribed youth for a French Canadian of the period. He was the manager of a local baseball team and a keen hockey player, took an undistinguished law degree from Laval and gravitated naturally to politics. There are rumors, unchecked like many others, that he supported conscription in the First World War. Whether or not for this reason, he was defeated in his first election for the provincial legislature, but was returned in 1927. He has been the representative—and part-time resident—of Three Rivers ever since, keeping the inhabitants happy with a fine baseball stadium, a nice swimming-pool and many other less concrete benefits, including, of course, the famous bridge that fell down several years ago.

In 1933, he took over the leadership of the Conservative Party from Camillien Houde, when the newly-elected Mayor of Montreal felt that the Depression problems of the metropolis might become a full-time job. The circumstances of the secret transfer left, however, a furious antagonism between the two men, which persisted for many years to the detriment of no one but the ordinary inhabitants of Montreal. Two years later, Duplessis formed his *Union Nationale* from moribund Conservatives, dissident Liberals and unattached Nationalists, held them together long enough to end old Taschereau's sixteen years of Liberal power, amidst blood-curdling attacks on the corruption and nepotism of *Les Canneux* (grandees who walk with canes—like Duplessis today).

The first Duplessis term was something of a period piece, a grotesquely parochial, wildly hilarious "government", largely carried on in hotel suites amidst numerous scandals, martinis, attendant ladies and bright red herrings—rather like Mitch Hepburn's contemporary regime in Ontario. It closed down in 1939 with a landslide victory for the Liberals, campaigning with all-out Ottawa support against *Union Nationale's* reckless anti-war attitude and a provincial debt which had been doubled in three years. The one real hang-over from this binge was the Padlock Law—a propaganda stunt, which was to be revived in more dangerous circumstances.

In 1944, Duplessis came back, it is often said, a changed man. He had completely given up drinking on the doctor's orders and was forsaking other pleasures. He was, too, more sensible about his choice of people. Attacks on *les Anglais* and *les Trustards* still echo with increasing hollowness. But, in fact, his government became more and more truly *bleu.*

It is often overlooked that Duplessis was restored in 1944, not only in opposition to the Liberals under Adelard Godbout, but in opposition to the anti-capitalist *Bloc Populaire*, with its dream of a Laurentian state. The vast capital which has gone into the development of the province ($7½ billion between 1948 and 1954 alone) owes something to the encouragement and "moderation" of the Duplessis regime.

Whether he could—and should—have demanded a higher price for his vast concessions and whether this kind of exploitation is the best way of developing the province is a controversial issue (and a real issue). The new Liberal leader, Georges Lapalme, has been making much of the "give-away" to the Iron Ore Company of Canada and other interests.

What is the case against Duplessis? He is not, it is generally conceded, a personally corrupt man. Indeed, in his disinclination "to give thought for the morrow" he compares very favorably with many other Canadian political leaders. And though he is not exactly favorable to criticism, it is true, he is at least ready to engage all comers. "With good government there is no need of an opposition," he once joked. But would Premier Manning, for instance, or even C. D. Howe have seen anything funny about such a remark?

Critics get fired from their jobs, hostile organizations are financially victimized. But who is to blame? Usually "someone" thinks it might be bad for his business if someone else says or does something to which Duplessis might take exception. This is the corruption of democracy more than the suppression of liberty—an atmosphere thickened by charges of electoral frauds and by loose parliamentary control of appropriations.

Duplessis has left himself open to most criticism on this score, too, where the interests are involved of those who smugly congratulate him on his "tolerance" towards the Protestant minority and carefully avoid "interference" by their Montreal businesses. His treatment of the strikers in the 1949 asbestos strike only served to deepen the antagonism of the Quebec industrial workers.

Duplessis can—and does—go after the odd businessman or priest. He can take on Archbishop Charbonneau, with some claim to success, and more recently the president of the Anglo-Canadian Pulp and Paper Company. But there is little he can do to change their basic policies in the long run. For having no real philosophy of government, he is, indeed, little more than a "go-between", and a manipulator, in the style of the traditional city "boss". The Corporations will continue to finance both parties—and the Church will have its representatives in several camps.

The real charge against Duplessis is that he has let himself be overtaken by events. The rapid industrialization of a backward province, to which in some measure he has contributed, has brought immense social problems—of health and housing, of law and, above all, of education. He leaves a potentially dangerous vacuum which more fanatical men may exploit, especially if there is an economic setback. This is the charge made by the unofficial opposition in Quebec which is represented by the leaders of the Catholic unions, by papers like *Le Devoir* and by some of the forward-looking clergy—most notably Father Lévesque. This opposition is much more lively than the official parliamentary opposition in Quebec, and a good deal more stimulating than the critics of the prevailing order in other parts of Canada. Liberty may get pushed around in Quebec, but it is in no danger of suffocating from complacency. And for this a little of the credit must go, paradoxically, to the provocative Chief.

André Laurendeau, "La Théorie du roi nègre," *Le Devoir*, July 4, 1958. (tr.)

The Negro King

Last Friday Mr. Maurice Duplessis brutally expelled Mr. Guy Lamarche, a *Le Devoir* journalist, from his office.

The reporter was attending the Prime Minister's press conference. He had not made a gesture nor spoken a word. He was simply there. It was enough to unleash Mr. Duplessis' anger. "Out" the Prime Minister screamed at him. Believing that he was exercising a usual right in a democratic country, the reporter from *Le Devoir* refused to obey. Mr. Duplessis had him expelled by a Provincial Police constable.

Three groups of journalists have since protested this act. They spontaneously recognized its gravity. A reporter "duly mandated by his paper to attend the press conference" of the Prime Minister must be able to "freely exercise his trade." These are most moderate words to describe the basic principle.

On the other hand the newspapers themselves have been very philosophical in their writings. With the exception of about two of them, they have written nothing. We will not insult them by concluding that they were not affected. They are the natural guardians not only of freedom of expression but that which renders it possible and protects it: notably, free access to sources of information. As a consequence the expulsion of a reporter from a press conference to which all of them had been theoretically invited could not but cause them alarm. Let us say that they were better able to contain their indignation than reporters were.

If Mr. Duplessis amuses himself by practising exclusion everyone knows that some day or other he may become the victim of them [*sic*]. Who will stop him from repeating against another newspaper his act against the *Le Devoir* reporter? In this case it was a press conference: within the same postulate, tomorrow it could be parliamentary debates.

And what is this postulate? Arbitrariness. We sincerely believe that Mr. Duplessis considers power as a personal possession. He disposes of it as he pleases. His friends obtain favours. Friendly counties receive particular consideration. Opposition deputies in the Assembly have but half rights, according to him. He treats them as if they had not been as legitimately elected as were the majority party.

Mr. Duplessis appears to believe that it is just and legitimate to starve the opposition, be it of jobs or roads, schools or bridges; only favourites are served. He has just applied this principle to newspapers: according to him an adversary is not worthy of hearing him. He chooses among newspapers those that are loyal and begins to exclude others.

This arbitrariness runs counter to democracy and the customs of a parliamentary regime. . . .

Usually the Anglophones are more

sensitive than we are to all infringements upon freedom. This is why Mr. Duplessis has a bad press outside of Quebec. Attacks on him in Ontario and Manitoba are not always inspired by the latter doctrine: old "race" and language prejudices are often given full voice. But we would err in explaining everything in terms of ethnic prejudices. The British have little by little gained political freedom; they are by habit more sensitive to threats to it.

Usually, we say, for in Quebec this tradition seems singularly anemic. This is so if we use Anglophone newspapers comments on Quebec events as criteria.

If it is a gag imposed in Ottawa by a majority then as a chorus all newspapers protest and it's a fine kettle of fish. The government, the Anglophone newspapers write with reason, (including those of Quebec), violates important parliamentary freedom. Whipped-up by newspapers, public opinion rumbles. This matter contributes to the Government's defeat: it's the pipeline affair.

In the Legislative Assembly of Quebec such incidents are common coin: our English language newspapers submit without protest. Why?

Guy Lamarche's expulsion last Friday is hard to swallow. English newspapers begin with silence. The day before yesterday, *The Gazette,* in the middle of an article sympathetic to the Government, registers the most minor protest imaginable. Yesterday, the *Star* declared Mr. Duplessis' gesture awkward, but does not judge it wrong. Why? . . .

Anglophone journals of Quebec behave like the British in an African colony.

The British have political sense: they rarely destroy the political institutions of a conquered country. They dominate the negro king but they allow him fantasies. On occasion they permit him to cut off a few heads: these are the mores of the country. One thing never comes to their minds, and that is to demand that the negro king conform to the high moral and political standards of the British.

The negro king must collaborate with and protect British interests. This collaboration assured, everything else goes by the boards. The kinglet violates democratic rules. Nothing else is expected from a primitive. . . .

I do not attribute these sentiments to the English minority of Quebec. But things occur as if a few of its leaders believe in the theory and practice of the negro king. They forgive the leader of the natives of Quebec, Mr. Duplessis, that which they would not tolerate from one of their own.

We see this currently in the Legislative Assembly. We saw it in the last municipal election. It has just been verified in Quebec.

The result is a regression of democracy and parliamentarianism, an uncontested reign of the arbitrary, a constant collusion of Anglo-Quebec finance with that which is most rotten in the politics of this province.

Pierre Laporte, *The True Face of Duplessis*, (Montreal, Harvest House, 1960), pp. 19-26. Reprinted by permission of Harvest House.

The Man

Maurice Duplessis was of middle height. He stood five feet nine. He was no Adonis but neither was he homely. Anyway, it is not in terms of homely or handsome that one thinks of some men. No one would bother asking if Winston Churchill or Charles De Gaulle are handsome men.

Duplessis had a broad forehead, cut by a line that at times was almost imperceptible, but which deepened when he smiled or was discontent. He had a good head of hair right up to his death. In fact at 69 he was still all pepper and salt even though he had aged terribly during his last five years.

The Duplessis nose in particular was a favourite subject of the cartoonists. It was not so abnormal as to draw great attention from people who met him. Still, it was not a nose that passed unnoticed, and it was underlined, thrown into relief, by two deep lines which ran down from the nostrils and disappeared at the edges of the mouth. Two other lines, less pronounced, formed parentheses around his dimpled chin.

Duplessis himself helped spread the legends that made his nose famous. He liked to talk about it. "It's not for nothing that my nose is so long," he often said, thereby trying to make people understand that he could not be fooled easily. . . .

Yet, what was really extraordinary in Maurice Duplessis' face was not his nose but his eyes. Surprisingly alive and intelligent, they were faithful mirrors of every disagreeable or agreeable impression that tossed about in his boiling brain.

When he laughed those eyes lit up his entire face. They gave off jocular yet half-devilish reflections whenever he was about to make one of his quips. People who worked around him and observed him knew in advance from those eyes if he was about to make a joke or to stump someone. When he was angry Duplessis' eyes flashed, something one did not see when this brilliant actor was simulating indignation or anger.

Sometimes his eyes had a worried look. Then he would frown, and would sink down in his chair as if asking himself what blow would befall him. This happened, for example, when Laurent Barré, the Minister of Agriculture, carried away in the heat of debate, would cry out: "What I am about to say I have not discussed with the Premier . . ." or: "Mr. Speaker, I will go even further . . ." The Minister committed a blunder on almost every such occasion.

Finally, Duplessis' eyes had indescribable but real magnetism. How often Members would criticize among themselves some attitude or stand of their leader and encourage one another to register a protest! They would decide to confront Duplessis squarely and tell him of their feelings. But once in front of him, they were without voice to express their grievance. They could not meet the eye of this leader of men.

Duplessis liked to dress well. He wore suits of sober tones and starched collars in the fashion of some years back. He took great care of his clothes and always made sure that his jacket and trousers were impeccably pressed. One day, as he was leaving for Three Rivers by car, he took his suit coat off and folded it carefully lest it lose its freshly pressed appearance on the trip. Then he put his overcoat on over his shirt. "I wouldn't want to drive into Trois-Rivières with a rumpled suit," he explained.

Duplessis looked ready to scream whenever a Member or a visitor walked in dressed loudly or sloppily.

Oddly enough, this natty man usually wore a beat-up fedora that contrasted amazingly with the rest of his clothes. It was a well-worn hat. Duplessis explained this anomaly himself one day. He wore an old hat, he said, so as not to "displease the people".

"A hat is the first thing people notice. So, since they're inclined to think persons who dress too well are stuck up and haughty, it is a good idea, from an electoral point of view, to wear a hat nobody resents. A good old hat! Lets you get close to the people."

Those who lived in the shadow of the founder of the Union Nationale party knew that his hands—they were rather fine and delicate—gave away his thoughts. When he was in an impatient mood, they toyed in circular motion around the rim of his glasses. Or, the left hand would execute a rotating motion on the cap of the left knee.

When he spoke, Duplessis was sparing in his arm movements. His most frequent gesture was to spread out his arms as if to stress a statement or punctuate an attack. Often, his right hand rested in the palm of his left.

In these speaking stances, Duplessis' head played a more dominant role than his hands. He marked each major assertion with short, rhythmic jabs of the head.

Was Duplessis a great orator? If one analyzes only his sentences, his ideas, his vocabulary, his grammar, he was one of French-Canada's worst. He started sentences and then left them dangling in midair without finishing them. He repeated the same things over and over again. His vocabulary was amazingly restricted. He massacred grammar.

But since the oratorical art is chiefly the art of swaying the masses and influencing opinion, it may be said that Maurice Duplessis was a good orator.

Few speakers could dominate an audience as well as he could, spread enthusiasm for even abstract ideas, arouse passions against an opponent even over peccadillos.

Once he was in full oratorical flight, Duplessis gave the impression of standing on a springboard. Each phrase of the speech, each sentence, was accentuated by a forward-upward motion of considerable power. He would speak slowly, quietly, for a few minutes, preparing his audience, giving the impression of searching for a solid grip on some point. Then his voice would grow in volume. He would change to short punchy phrases, increasing delivery to machine-gun speed, and would wind up booming out great sweeping statements that swept the audience off its feet and drove his supporters into a frenzy. . . .

Duplessis never, or almost never, took a holiday. This stemmed, it is said, from two reasons. He figured a holiday was a waste of time, and he feared that if he went away for an extended period some terrible thing might happen back in

Quebec City. This man, who never had complete confidence in anyone, feared that his colleagues might jump at the opportunity to plot some dark deed or make some scandalous decision.

Duplessis departed—on the rare occasions he did leave—for a week at the most. He would go to the United States to attend the World Series. Once, he spent a brief holiday on a sunny West Indian island. When he left, he rarely thought it necessary to appoint an interim Premier. This led George Lapalme—named chief of the Quebec Liberals in 1950—to quip: "Mr. Duplessis has a portable government. He carries it in his brief case wherever he goes."

Duplessis hardly knew how to relax. He had two hideouts: his rooms at the Chateau Frontenac in Quebec City, and his office at the Legislature. He rose early, and was the first client of the hotel's barber shop almost every morning.

He went to the Legislature about 8:30 a.m.

For many years he walked there, accompanied by his bodyguard, a nice enough fellow whose main job seems to have been to pick up the latest jokes going the rounds of the city and tell them to the Premier.

Once his day was over, Duplessis would return to the Chateau where he remained until the following morning. He had a fine record collection, which he played full volume. A great newspaper reader, he went through stacks of them every evening. As he finished each, he would throw it to the floor around him and there they would lay, crumpled and pell-mell. They piled up . . . but no one had the right to pick them up except his extremely devoted secretary, Miss Auréa Cloutier. She went to his rooms occasionally to clean up the place.

Besides reading the newspapers, Duplessis listened to as many radio and television newscasts as he could.

The man had admirers, courtiers, extremely devoted supporters, even what one might describe as veritable slaves, but . . . no friends.

He rarely saw anyone at the Chateau Frontenac, except to talk politics. Sometimes he would invite some noted person, who wished to see him, to breakfast. The purpose of such a meeting was to avoid the newspapers getting wind of it. Or, in some cases, because he did not wish a visitor to wait in the ante-room at his Legislature office.

Duplessis lived the life of a hermit. While he loved animation and activity during the day, he fiercely guarded his privacy in the evening. This was true of the last fifteen years of his life. It is said that his earlier years were more lively. . . .

This mixture of noise and silence, of feverish activity and quiet solitude depicts Maurice Duplessis fairly well—as a man who always refused to let others see him exactly as he was.

Duplessis was vigorous as few men are. His powers of recuperation were prodigious. Sometimes, in the evening, he would look withered, empty. A few hours of sleep and he would emerge the next day fresh, his eyes alert, appearing his usual aggressive self. "I am dangerously well," he replied to those who asked after his health.

For thirty years he operated like a dynamo, displaying a volume of energy—often for no reason at all—that would have quickly killed another man with a weaker constitution. Duplessis died on the job, as he would have wished, having refused, to the last minute, to heed any possible inner fears of those who urged him to see a doctor. Already stricken by the disease which was to carry him off, he refused to stop. Impatiently, he would snap to those who tried to slow him down: "I am no young doll!"

Shortly afterwards, at Schefferville, in the Ungava territory, he died of a massive cerebral haemorrhage.

This man who had been adulated, who received ovations as few other Quebec politicians ever had, this man of the crowds, died almost alone in one of the wildest and most deserted areas of the province.

Even in death he illustrated the passions which he aroused in the hearts of men. His friends declared that he died in the heart of the "empire" he had opened to civilization and progress. His opponents whispered that through some twist of fate, he had died on the scene of his worst treason.

François-Albert Angers, "La fin d'un Régime?" *L'Action Nationale,* October 1959, pp. 91-94. (tr.) Reprinted by permission of *L'Action Nationale.*

In the End was Duplessisme

Prime Minister Duplessis, like his illustrious predecessor Alexandre Taschereau, and undoubtedly for somewhat the same reasons—the length of his mandate—had become . . . the gad-fly in the bonnet of his political opponents. For several years all battles had centred on his person, his methods of action and his ideas. Some people ardently desired his disappearance from the political scene; it would surely mark the end of a régime, a sort of turning point in history. And now he has suddenly died on the job, without ever being defeated, without suffering the agony of a long illness and the humiliation that would have befallen him had he been forced to resign. In short, even in death, everything occurred as if he himself had planned his fate. Struck down in full stride, he was given a grandiose State funeral attended by statesmen from across the nation. He enters history on both feet, almost a legend in his own time; and, in their own way, his opponents perpetuate his memory by continuing to speak of *Duplessisme.* But is it really the end of a régime?

In one respect, namely, if we consider his successor, the answer appears to be yes. The journalists and civil servants to whom we have spoken are unanimous in saying that the entire atmosphere in Quebec has changed. A man who focussed everything on himself, who insisted on knowing everything and on doing everything in his government, has been succeeded by someone with a completely different temperament, someone who at the moment seems rather to have the qualities of a great administrator, whereas even M. Duplessis' opponents admitted that he had the qualities of a great politician. However, this is a somewhat superficial aspect of the matter.

The end of a régime generally meant the end of a political system which some people sincerely abhorred and others simply denounced in order to defeat Mr. Duplessis, to take his place, and to do more or less the same things. The end of a régime also meant . . . the departure of a man who, rightly or wrongly, used every means at his disposal to prevent the acceptance of certain policies and certain federal subsidies. And outside Quebec: the disappearance of someone who had been made out to be a kind of anti-Christ, the incarnation of French Canadian nationalism and of the resistance to federal encroachments, that is to say, the insidious pursuit of a policy of rehabilitating the Union through a Confederation that the English-Canadian Unionists had no more accepted than the Separatists of Quebec. In short, various groups of people ardently desired his departure for very different and often irreconcilable motives. And even had he one day been beaten by a coalition of his opponents, that would have been a day when somebody somewhere was made a fool.

Those who ran the greatest risk of being duped were the ones . . . who called Duplessis the inventor of the system of electoral politics which he called *Duplessisme.* In fact, Mr. Duplessis merely perpetuated a body of practices which have always been widespread among us, both at the Federal and the provincial level. . . . If they are more nefarious here than elsewhere, it is owing to our peculiar position as a dominated group and to the fact that our politicians are selected by large national parties, that is to say, so as to eliminate craftily any man who believes too sincerely in the true interests of the French Canadian community, a belief which sometimes extends to the point of Irredentism. It is more than likely, if not certain, that Mr. Duplessis' death will not change this one bit. Reforms, if there are really any possible, must be carried out within an unsuitable historical framework; and if changes are to be made, they can only be affected if the new government leader has Mr. Duplessis' somewhat dictatorial temperament. . . .

In all justice to Mr. Duplessis and his reign, the objective observer of the future will not be able to avoid concluding that, under his leadership, the Union Nationale somehow dissociated itself, more than had any other traditional political party in Quebec, from the influence of national political parties and converted itself into a provincial political party capable of defending provincial interests. . . . On this point, Mercier is the only one to whom Duplessis might be compared; and we know that "high finance" quickly brought Mercier to heel and got rid of him. . . . Foreign financial powers still play a major rôle in the orientation of our politics. Mr. Duplessis, who knew his political history well . . . Mr. Duplessis, I repeat, (*a man*) who did not have the temperament of a reformer, but rather the temperament of a politician interested above all in retaining political power, was not the man to go further.

Suggested Reading

No definitive biography of Duplessis has yet been written. His personal papers, which are under the control of his sister, are not available for consultation. The same is true of another important set of documents: those of Paul Gouin. His papers are on deposit at the Public Archives of Canada in Ottawa, but access to them is restricted to permission from the depositor, Paul Gouin. Such permission was not obtainable for the purposes of the present work.

Most of the useful works on Duplessis have been used in this book of readings. Of particular value, with some reservations as to ideological propensities, is the multi-volume *Histoire de la Province de Quebec* by Robert Rumilly. The latest volumes concern Duplessis' first régime, his defeat and the war years. Personal memoirs, such as those of Antonio Barrette, and the forthcoming political autobiography of Georges Lapalme, and T. D. Bouchard's *Mémoires,* offer surprisingly few insights into the period or the man, Duplessis. Pierre Laporte's *True Face of Duplessis* and *Le Chef* by Leslie Roberts should be used with care since they are biased. Both writers are unable to disguise their admiration for the late Premier.

An extremely good study of French Canadian nationalism is Michael Oliver's *The Social and Political Ideas of French Canadian Nationalists, 1920-45,* (unpublished Ph.D. thesis, McGill University). Herbert Quinn's study *The Union Nationale: A Study in Quebec Nationalism,* (Toronto: University of Toronto Press, 1963), emphasises the electoral system of the Duplessis era rather than specific issues.

Newspapers and periodicals provide the best source material. In addition to the *Canadian Forum, Saturday Night,* the *Montreal Gazette* and *Montreal Star* used in this book, *Le Devoir, La Presse,* the now extinct *Montreal Herald,* and the *Montreal Matin,* the last a Union Nationale paper, contain interesting and useful materials. Two French language periodicals of extreme value are *L'Action Nationale* and *Relations*. The revolt of the intellectuals, the Trudeau, Pelletier group, will be found in *Cité Libre*.

Laval University's publication, *Relations Industrielles*, provides a good source of information on labour in Quebec. Surprisingly enough, the archives of the Fédération des Travailleurs du Québec contain little material on Duplessis, other than commonly known data. The *Ecole Sociale Populaire* publications, as well as the reports of the annual *Semaine Sociale*, contain a tremendous amount of information on the Roman Catholic Church's views of Quebec society and ideology from the 1920's on.

APPENDIX

PROVINCIAL ELECTIONS IN QUEBEC, 1935-1956

Year	Liberals Elected	% of Vote	U.N. Elected	% of Vote	Others
1935	48	50.2	16[1]	48.7[2]	26[3]
1936	14	41.8	76	57.5	
1939	70	54.2	15	39.2	1
1944	37	39.5	48	35.8	6
1948	8	38.3	82	51	2
1952	23	46	68	51.5	1
1956	20	44.5	72	52	

[1]—Union Nationale was not a party until 1936:16 elected as Conservatives.

[2]—Includes l'Action Libérale Nationale votes.

[3]—L'Action Libérale Nationale deputies.